AF262540

STRIKING A POSE

Anita Kunz

FRONT COVER

THE MUSICAL VISIONARIES

Bob Dylan, Frank Zappa & Leonard Cohen

Editor: Gary Groth
Proofreader: Kit Brash
Designer: Justin Allan-Spencer
Production: Paul Baresh
VP/Associate Publisher: Eric Reynolds
Publisher: Gary Groth

Visit Ms Kunz at: www.anitakunz.com

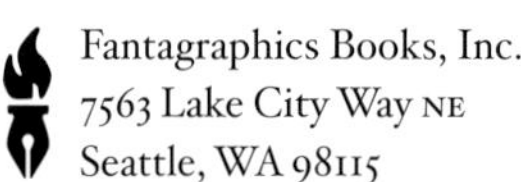

Fantagraphics Books, Inc.
7563 Lake City Way NE
Seattle, WA 98115

www.fantagraphics.com
facebook.com/fantagraphics
@fantagraphics.com

ISBN: 978-1-68396-883-2
Library of Congress Control Number: 2023935764
First Fantagraphics Books edition: Fall 2023
Printed in the Republic of Korea

STRIKING A POSE

A HANDY GUIDE TO THE MALE NUDE

Anita Kunz

FANTAGRAPHICS • SEATTLE, WA

The human figure is one of the most enduring themes in the visual arts, and figure drawing can be applied to fine art, portraiture, cartooning, comic book illustration, graphic novels, sculpture, medical illustration and other related areas.

Throughout art history, the nude female form has been ubiquitous. Women have long thought to have been the best models for artists. The males of our species seem to have been vastly neglected. Here then is a volume of sketches of the male nude.

This book is dedicated to art students everywhere who struggle with the challenges of drawing from the nude life model.

— *AK*

All drawings are pencil and watercolor sketches on 9.5″ × 14.75″ Barchan Green, handmade, Cambersand paper, with special thanks to Maureen and Simon Green.

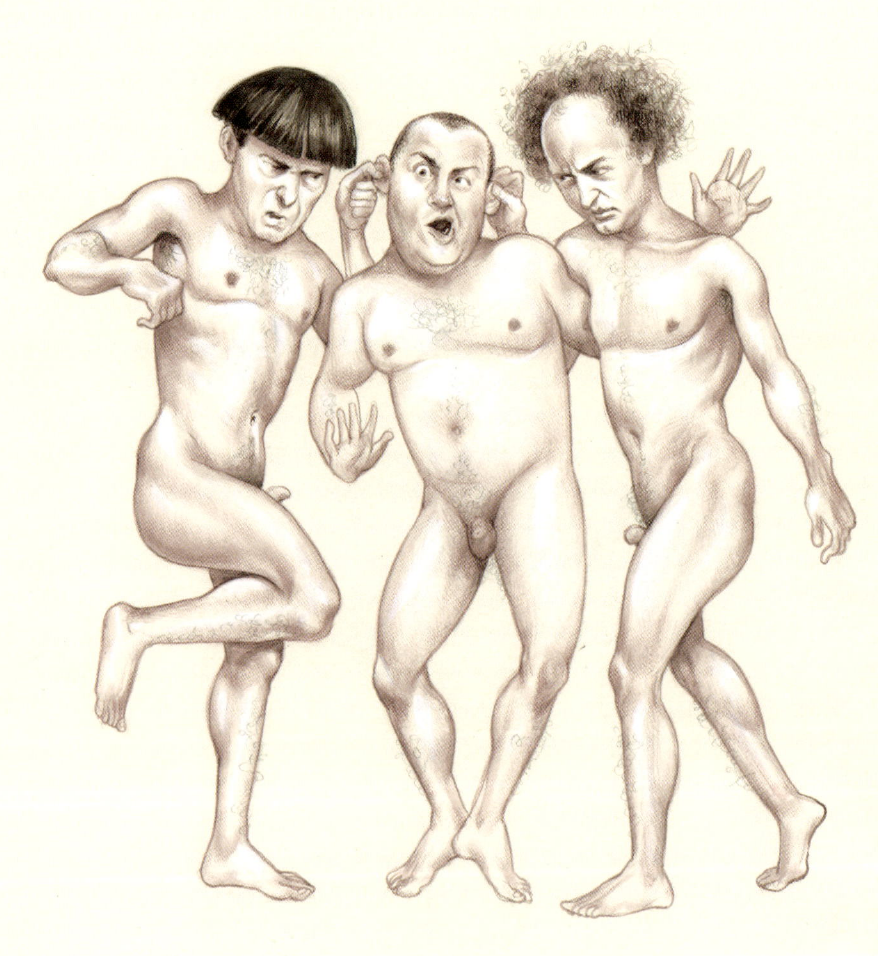

THE STOOGES

Moe, Curly & Larry

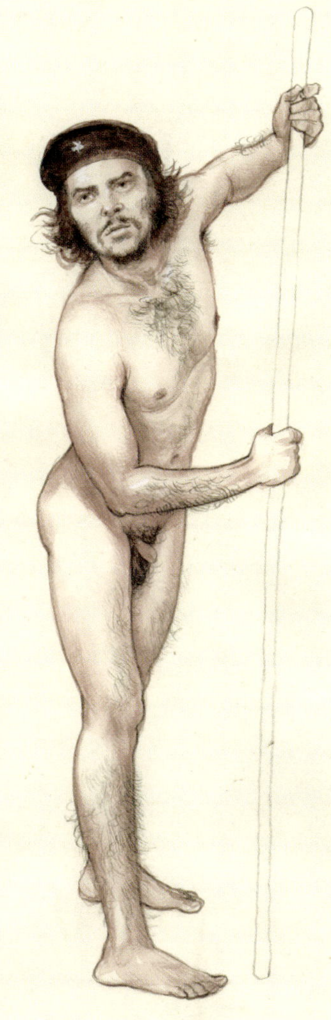

Che Guevara

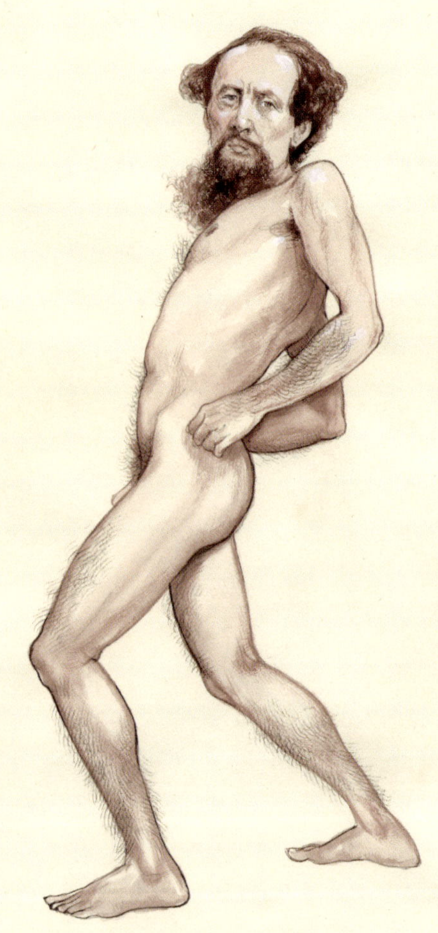

Charles Dickens

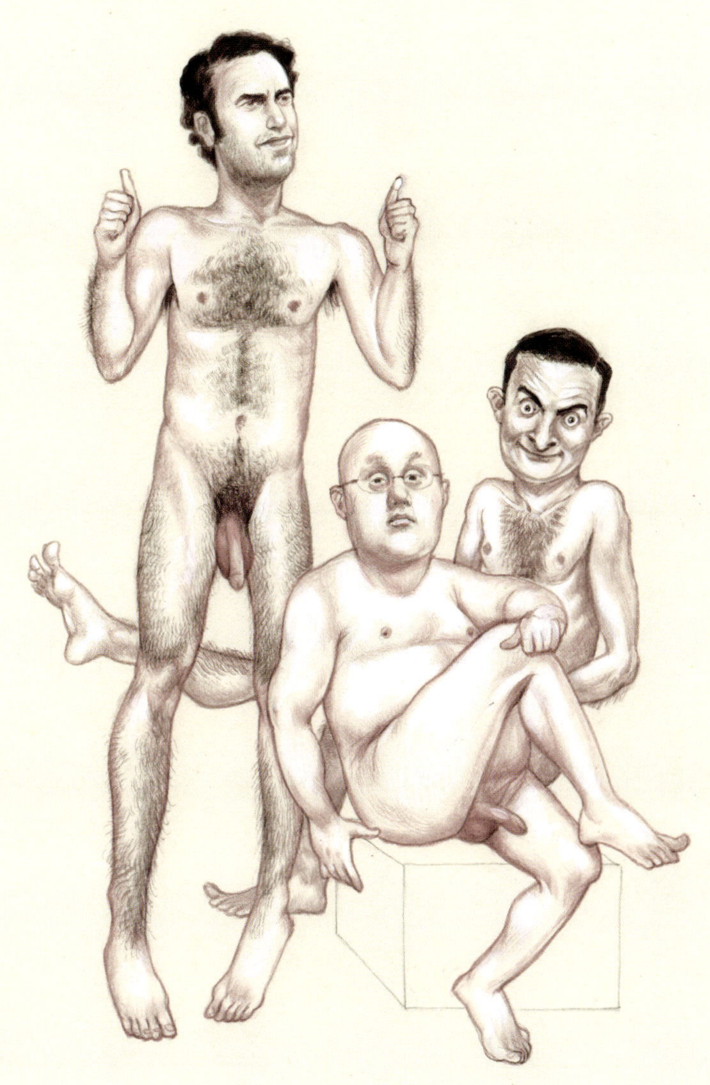

THE COMEDIANS

Sacha Baron Cohen, Matt Lucas & Rowan Atkinson

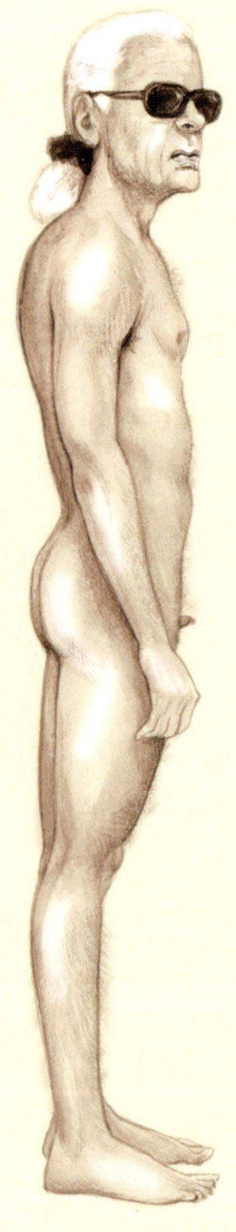

Karl Lagerfeld

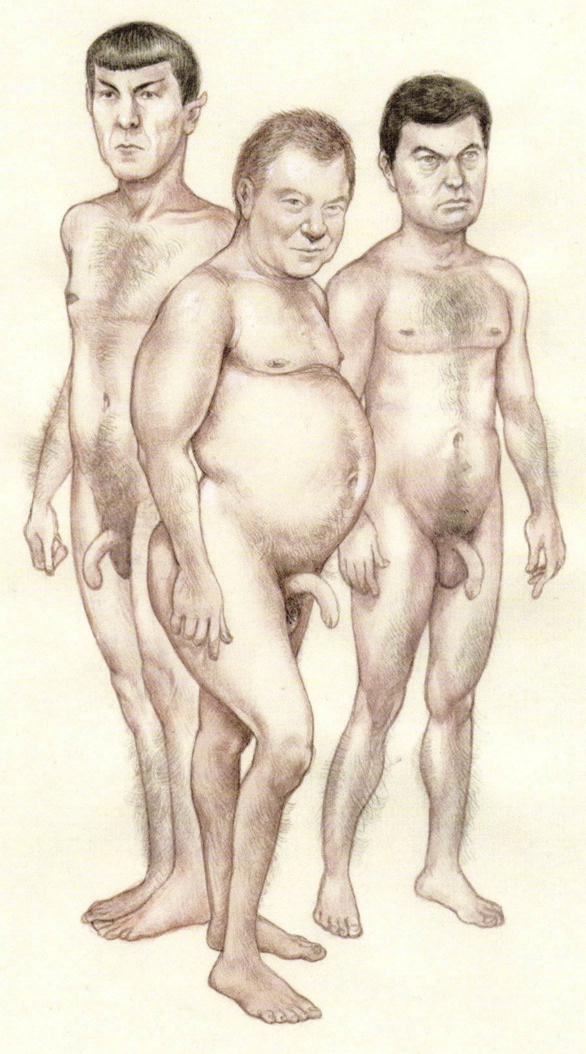

THE SPACE EXPLORERS

Leonard Nimoy, William Shatner & DeForest Kelley

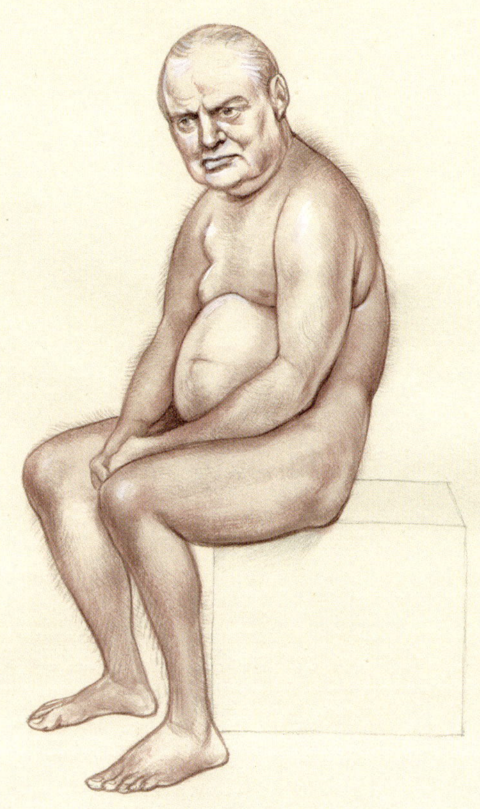

Winston Churchill

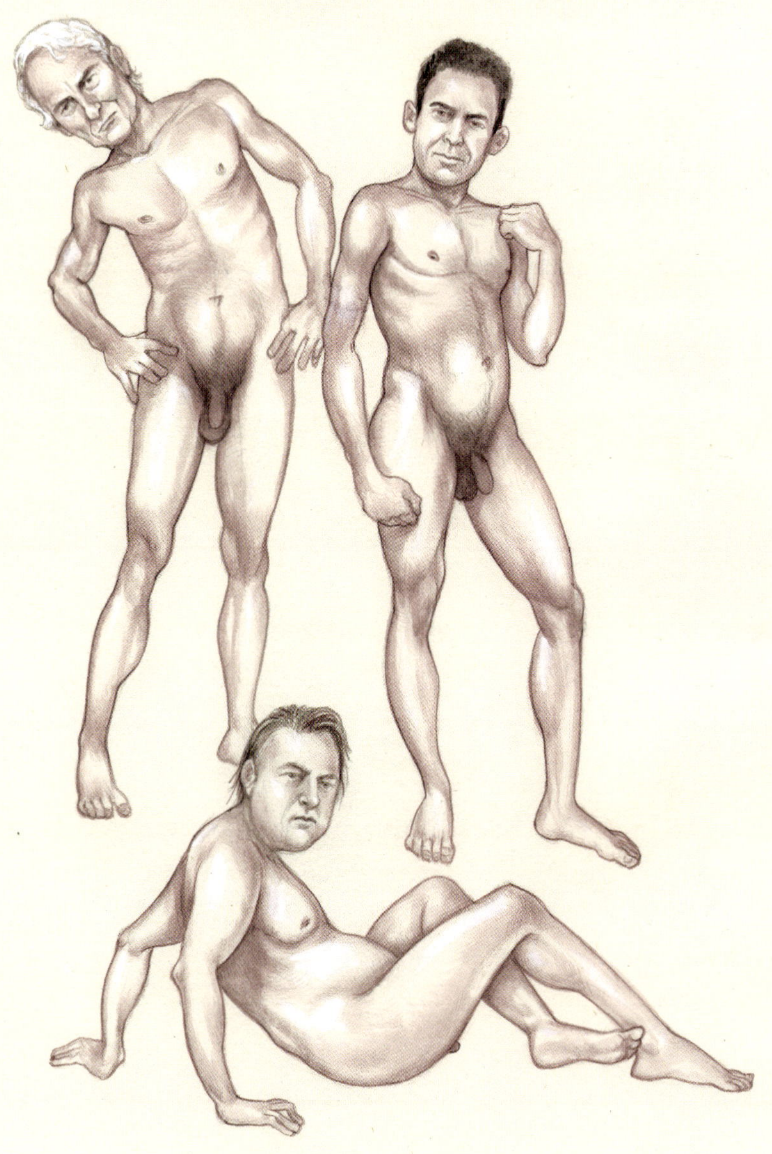

THE ATHEISTS

Richard Dawkins, Sam Harris & Christopher Hitchens

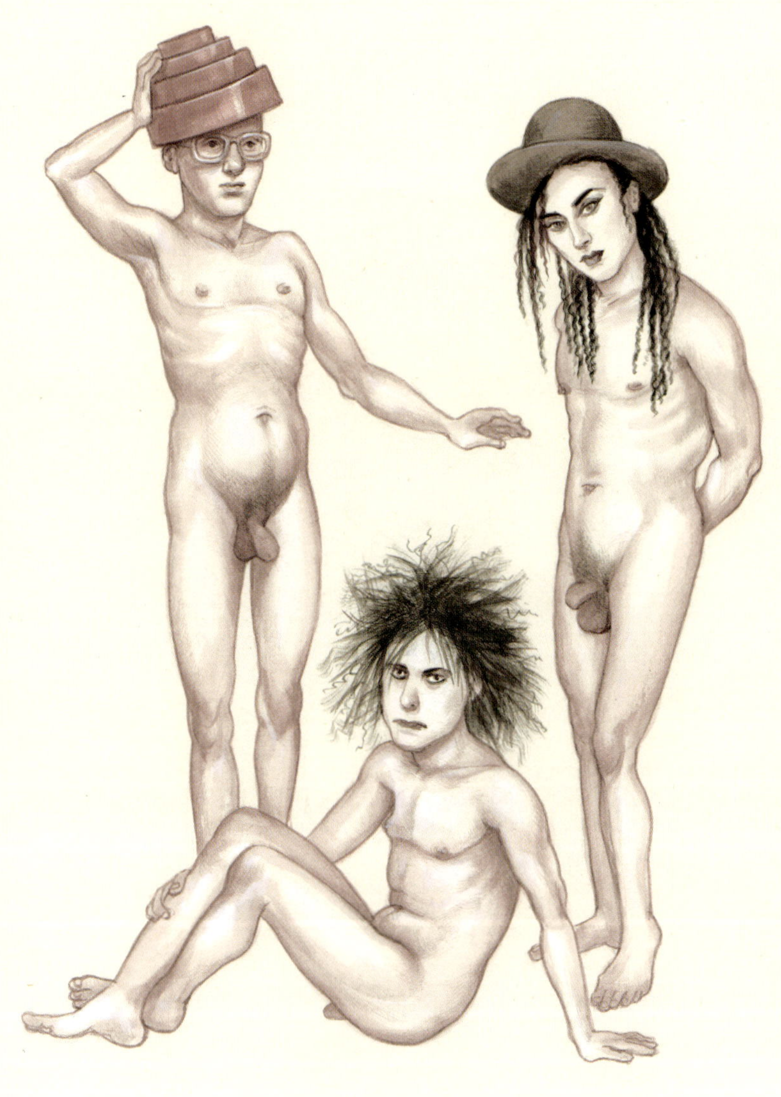

THE NEW WAVE

Mark Mothersbaugh, Robert Smith & Boy George

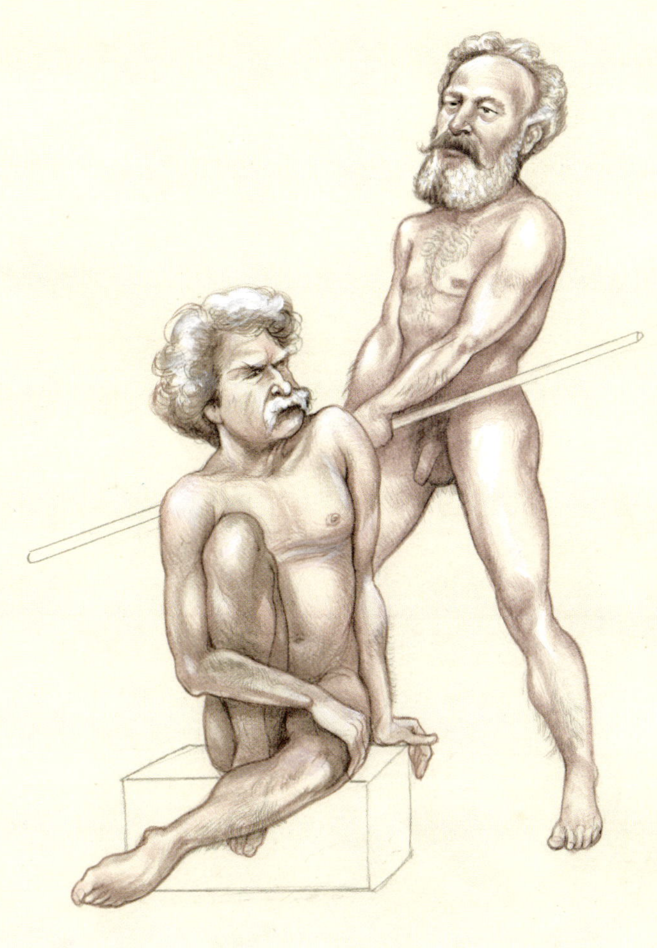

THE AUTHORS

Mark Twain & Jules Verne

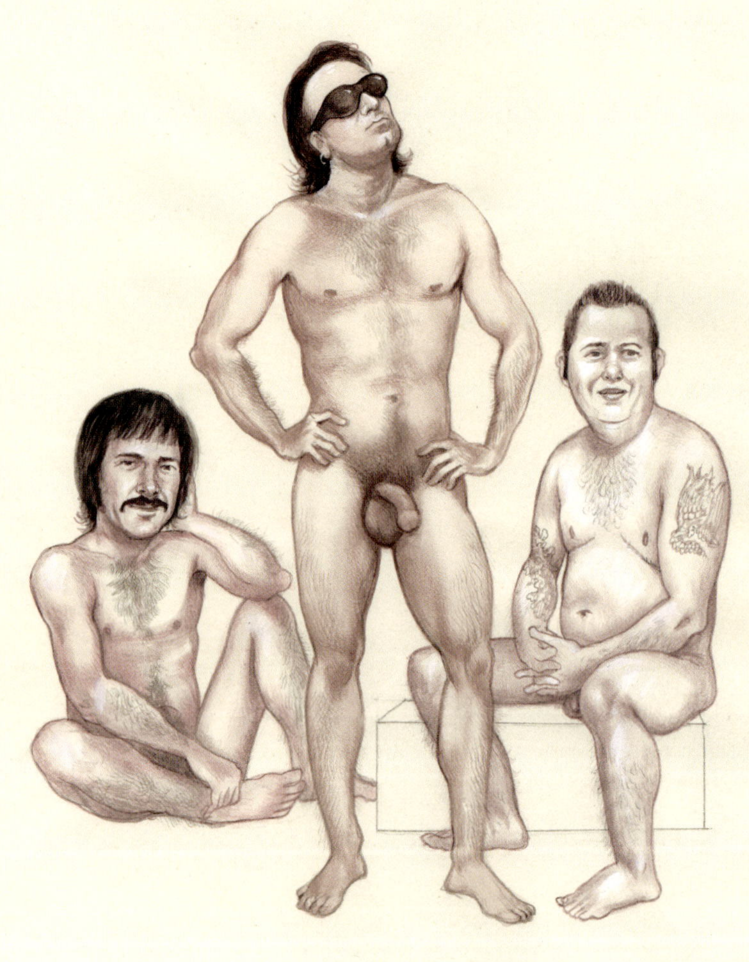

THE BONOS

Sonny Bono, Bono & Chaz Bono

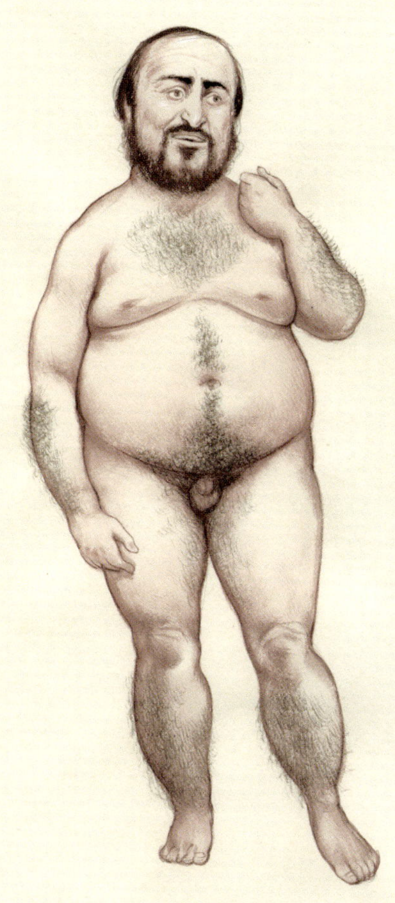

Luciano Pavarotti

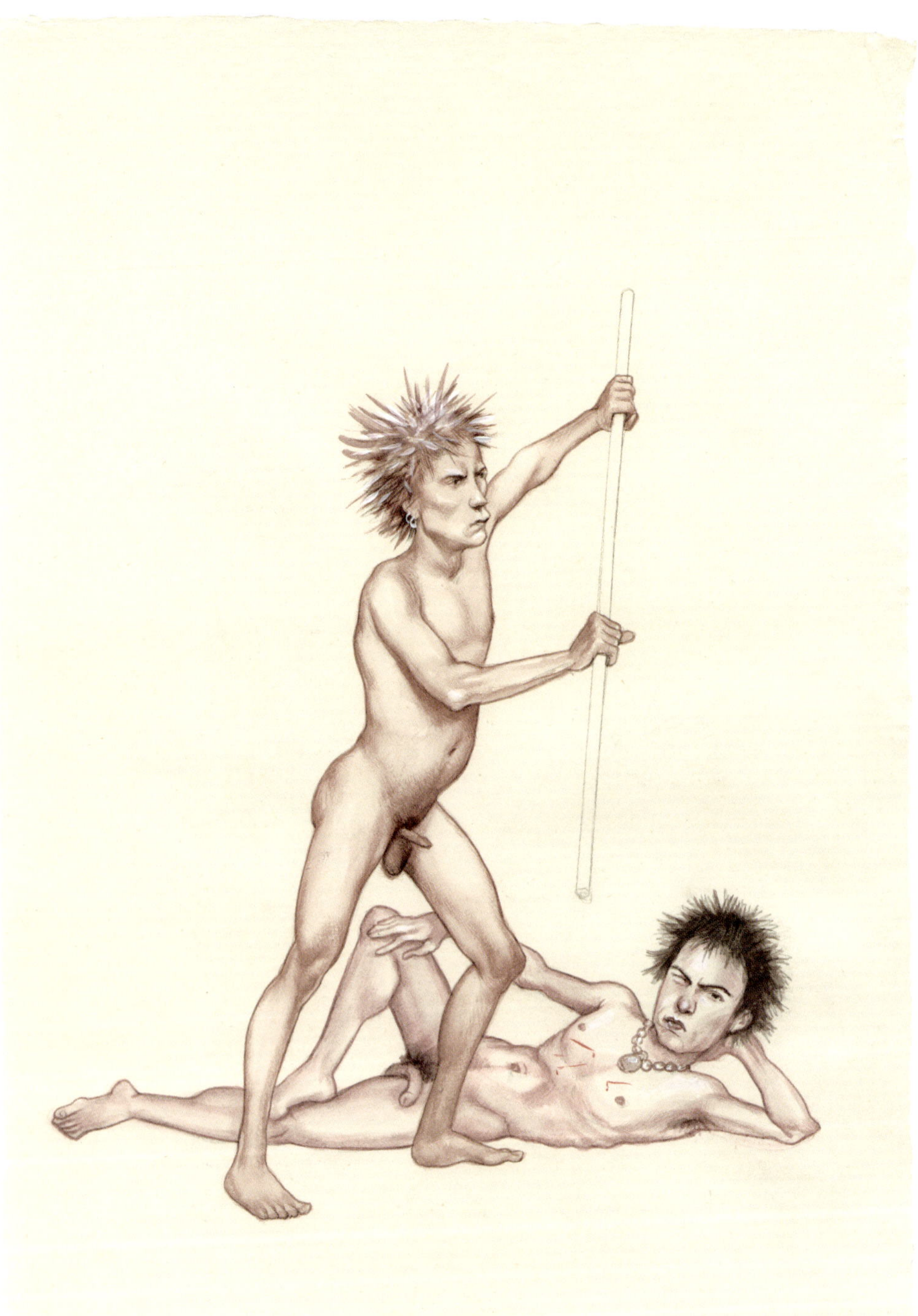

THE SEX PISTOLS

Johnny Rotten & Sid Vicious

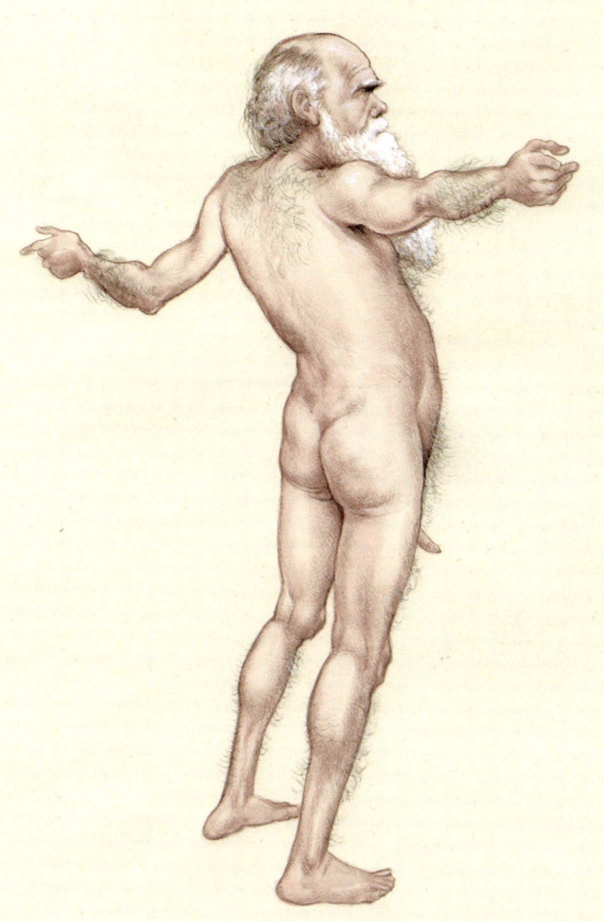

Charles Darwin

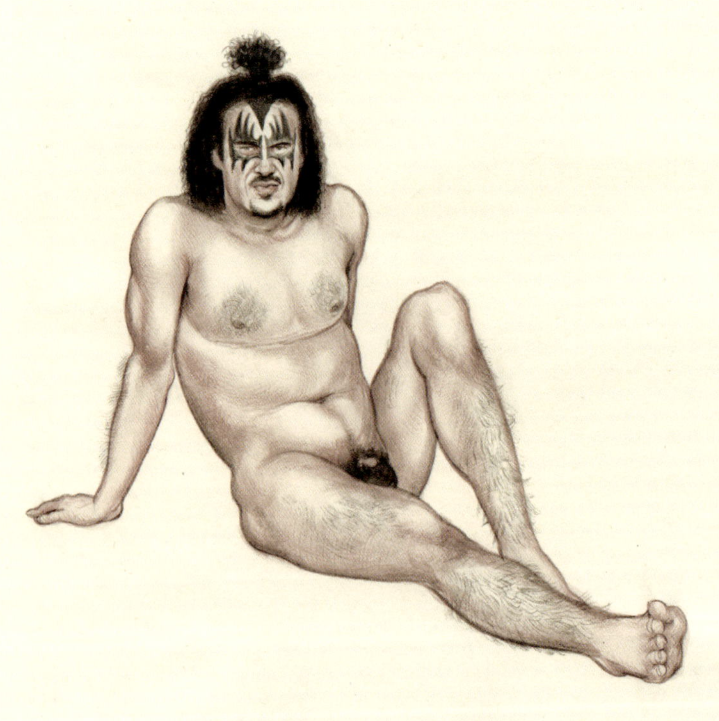

Gene Simmons

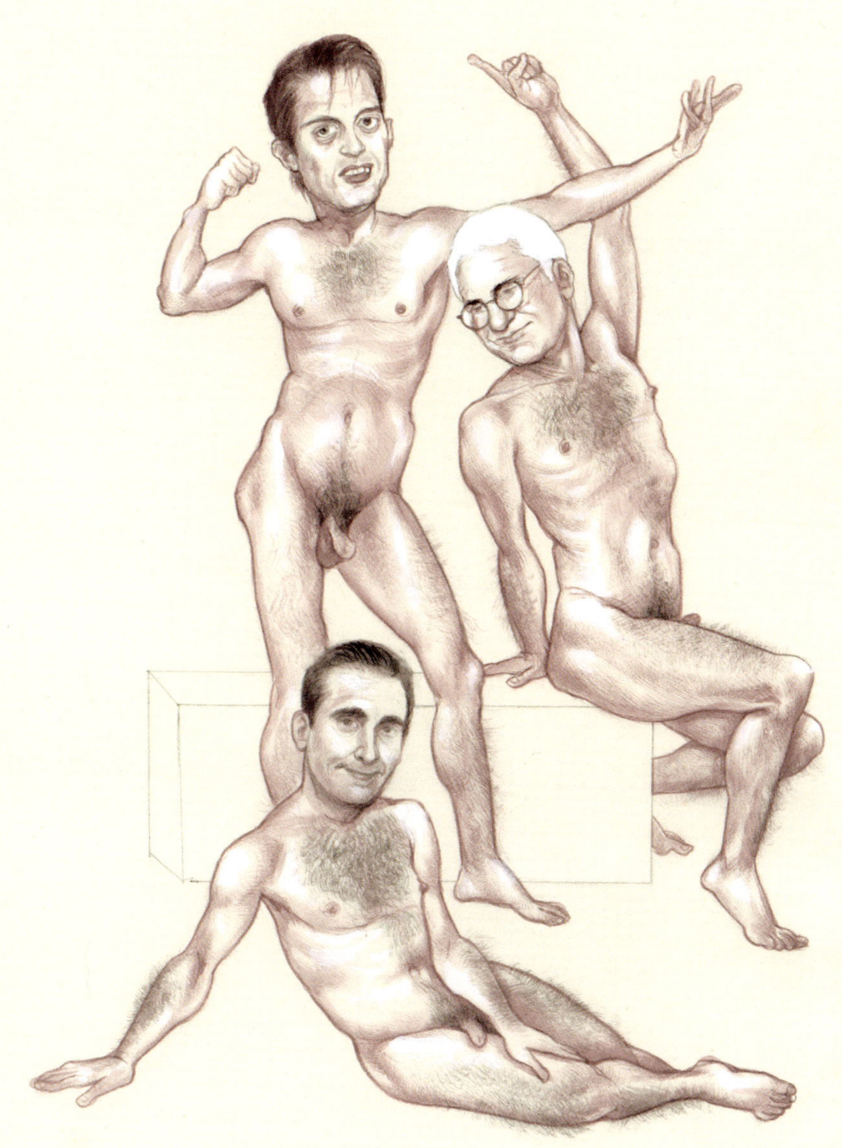

THE STEVES

Steve Buscemi, Steve Martin & Steve Carell

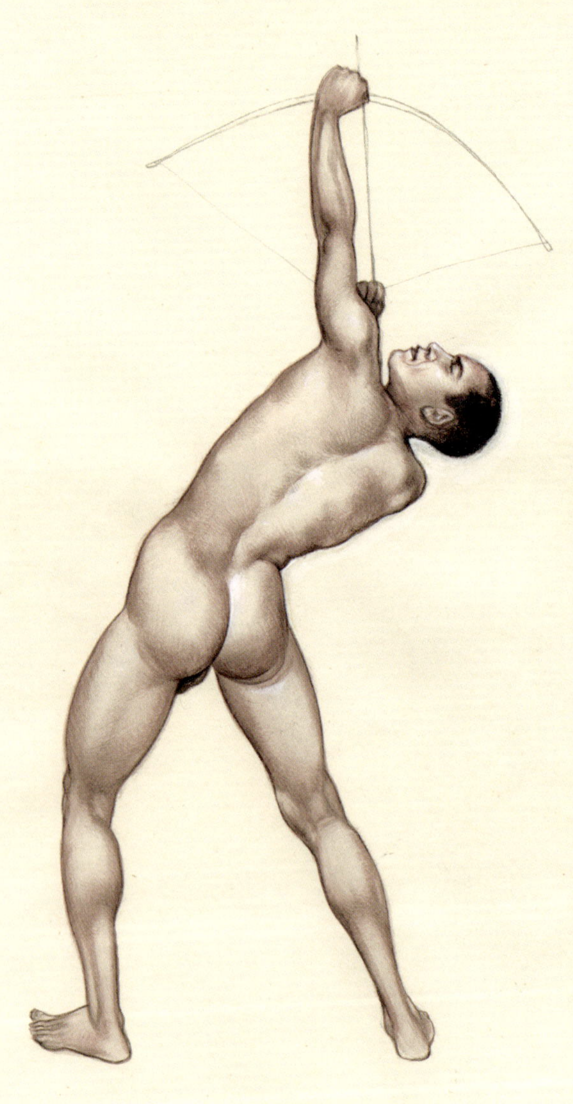

Barack Obama

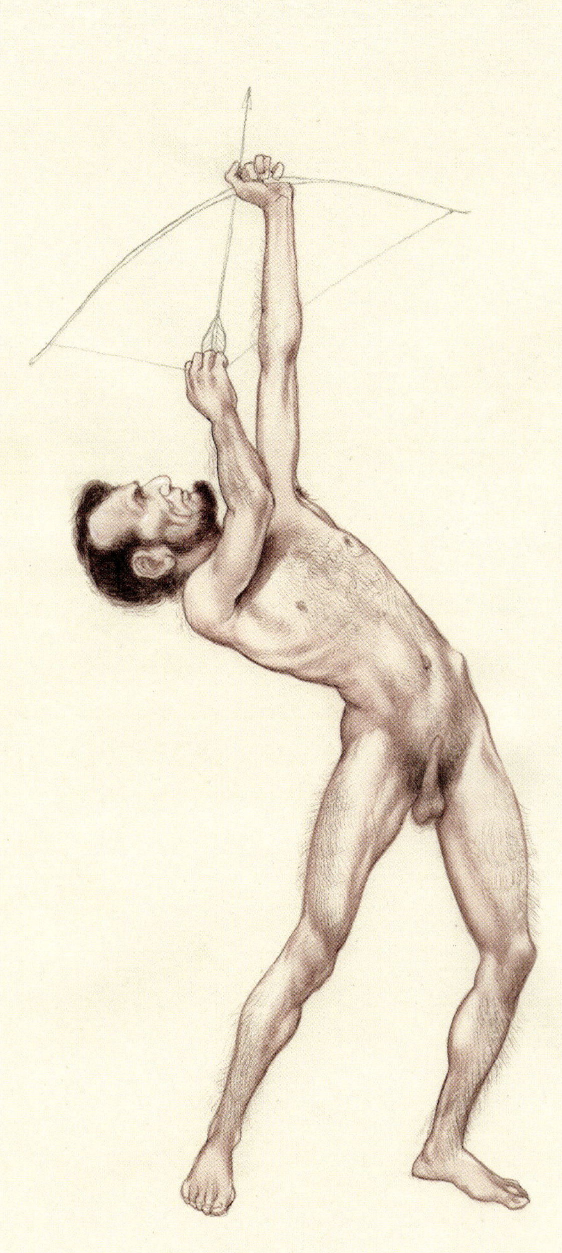

Abraham Lincoln

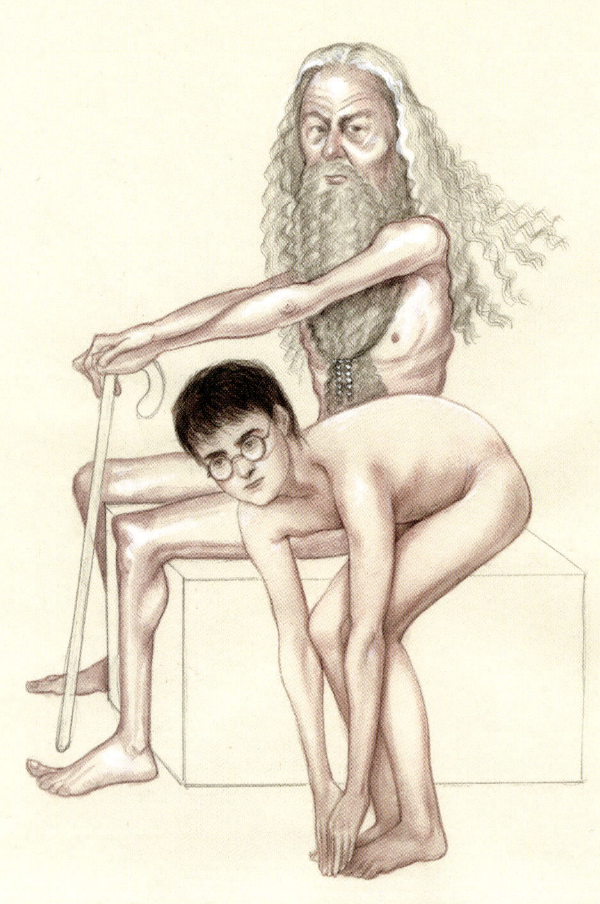

THE FANTASY ACTORS

Michael Gambon & Daniel Radcliffe

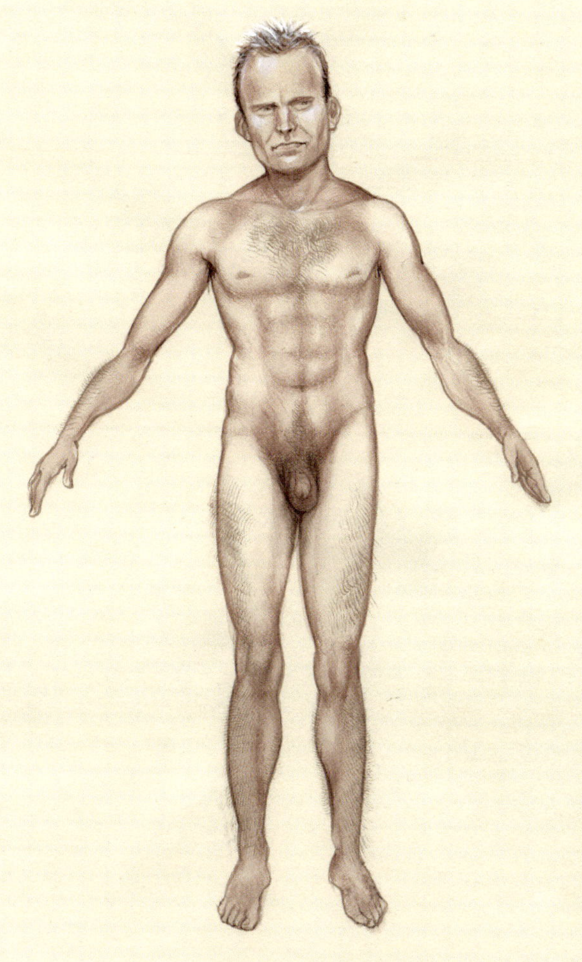

Sting

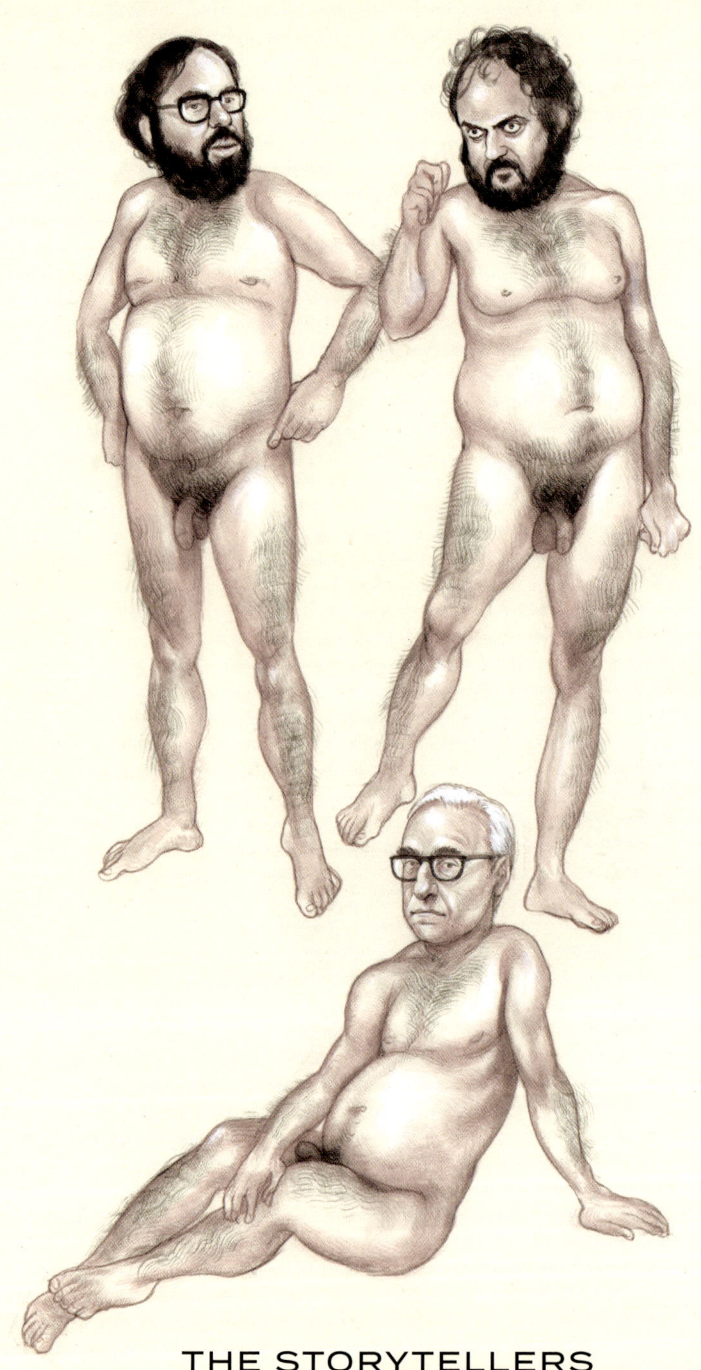

THE STORYTELLERS

Francis Ford Coppola, Stanley Kubrick & Martin Scorsese

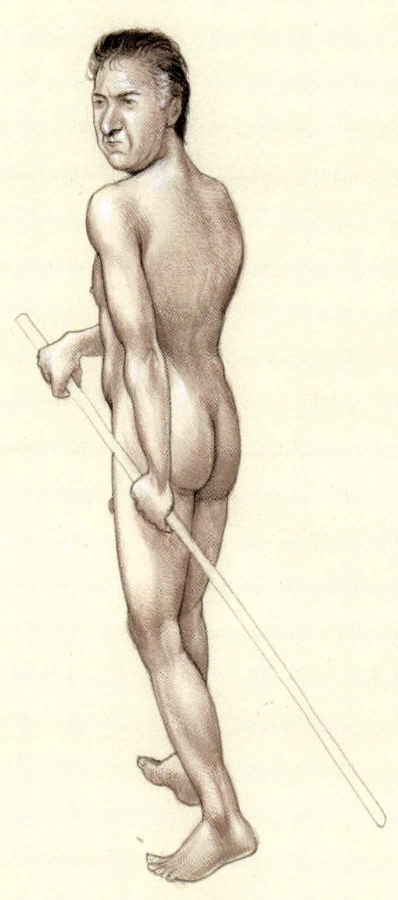

Dustin Hoffman

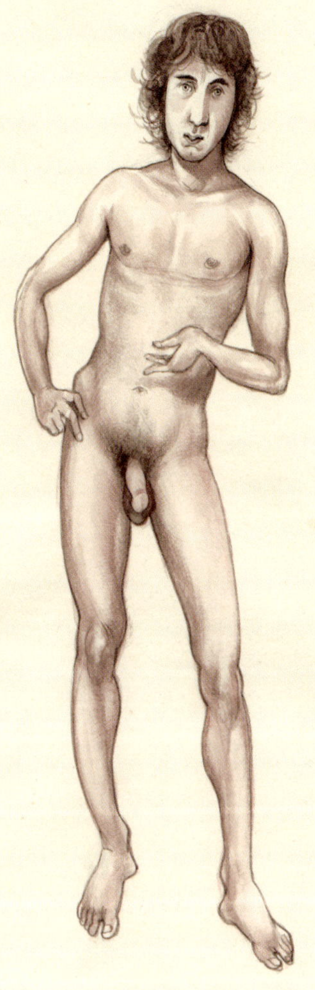

Pete Townshend

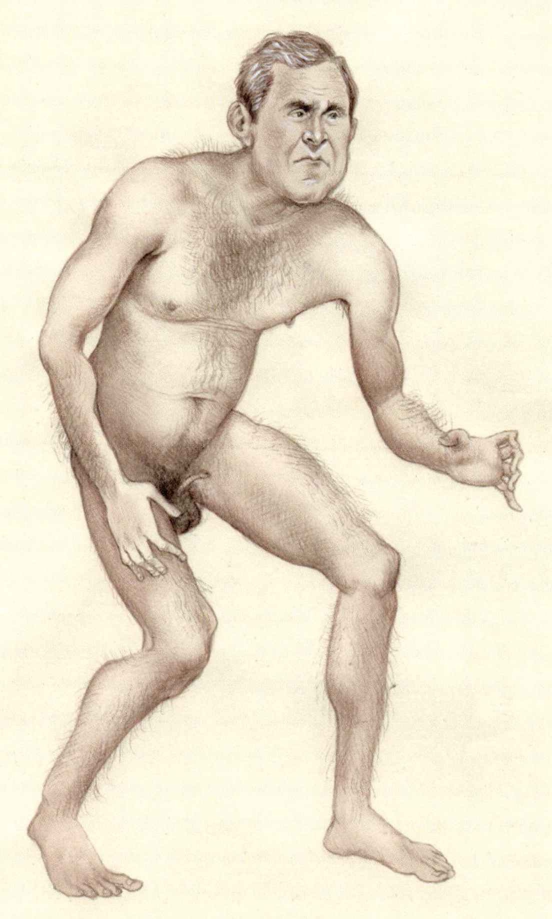

George W. Bush

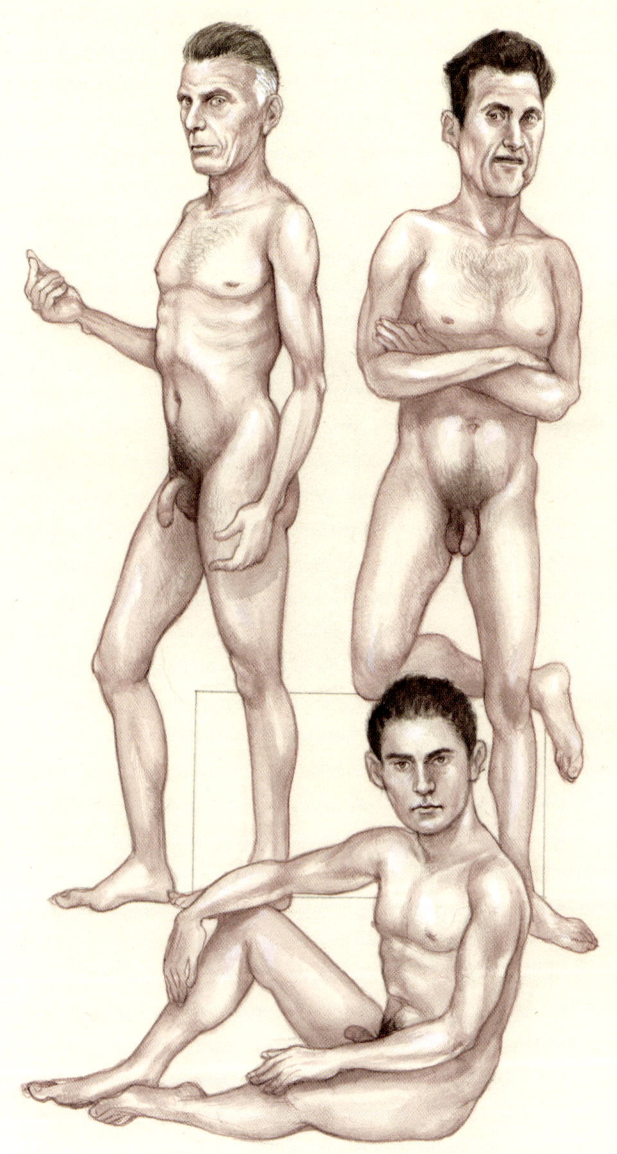

THE NOVELISTS

Samuel Beckett, George Orwell & Franz Kafka

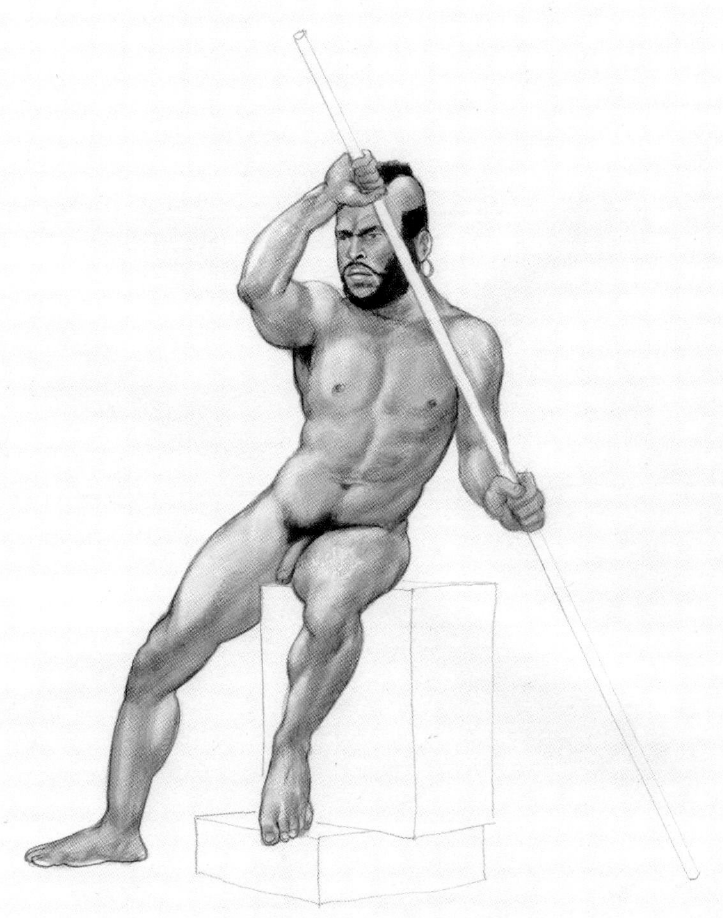

Mr. T

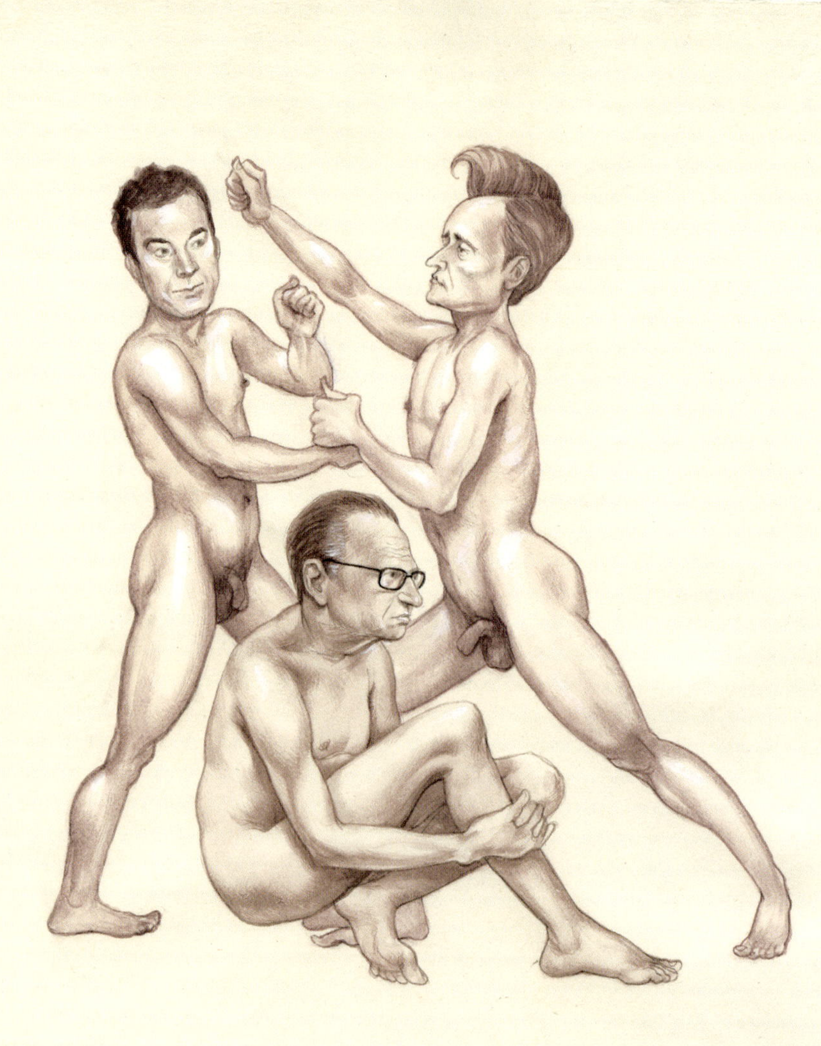

THE TALK SHOW HOSTS

Jimmy Fallon, Larry King & Conan O'Brien

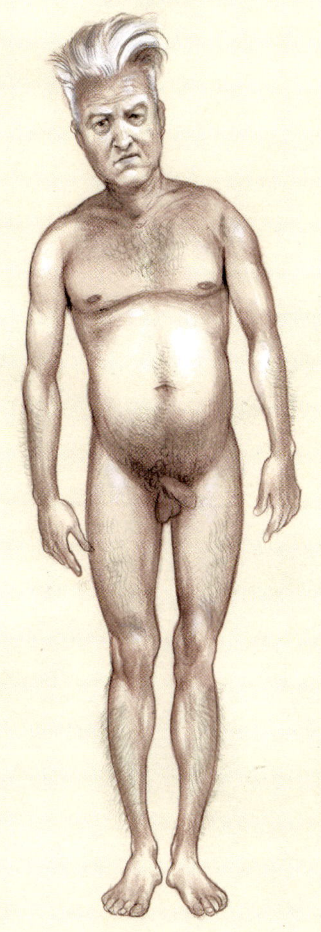

David Lynch

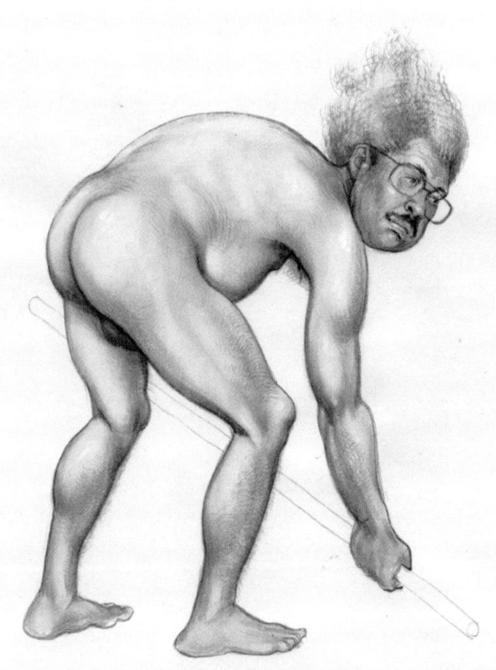

Don King

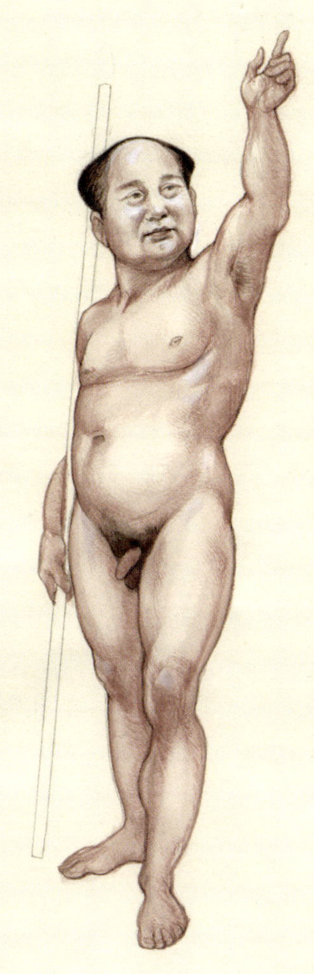

Mao Zedong

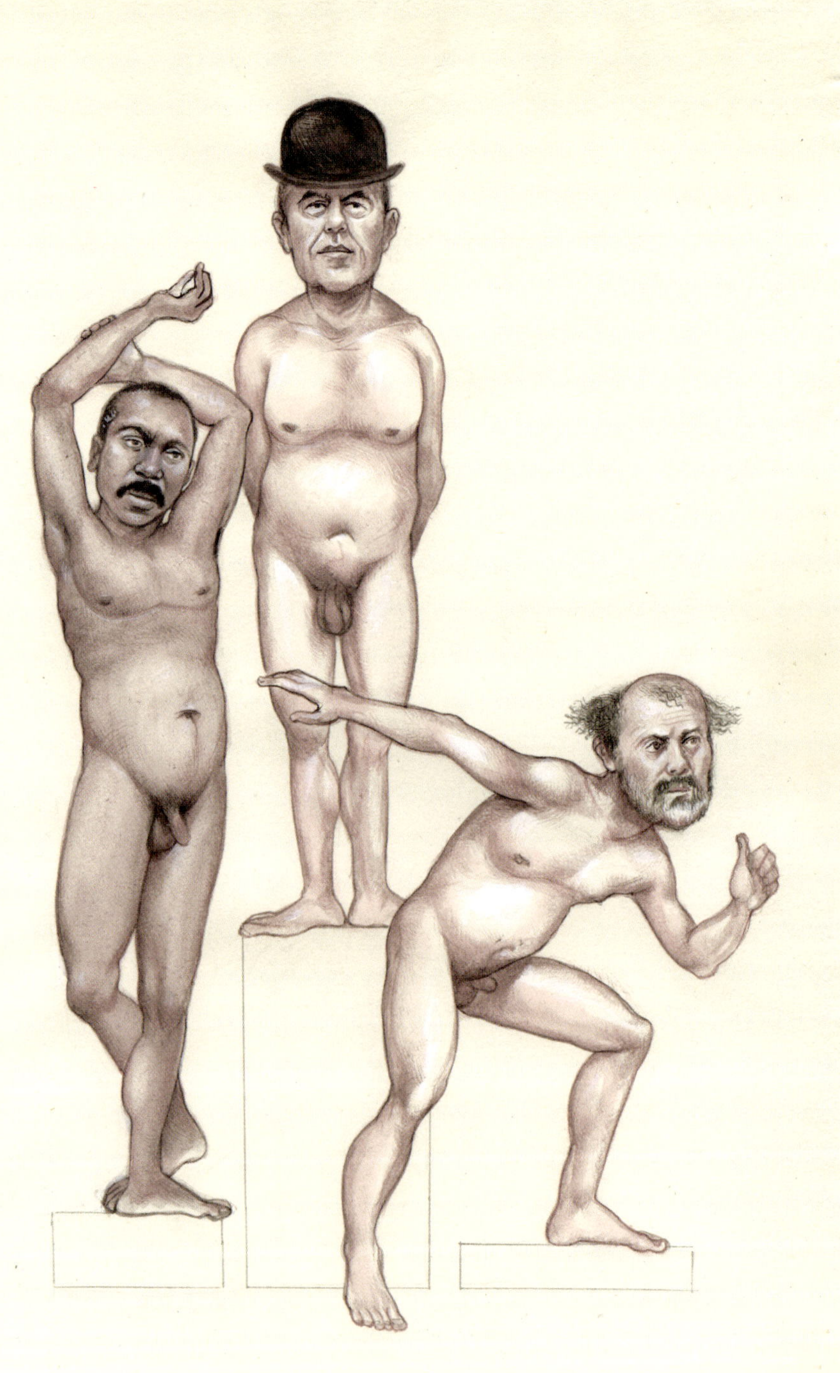

THE PAINTERS

Jacob Lawrence, René Magritte & Gustav Klimt

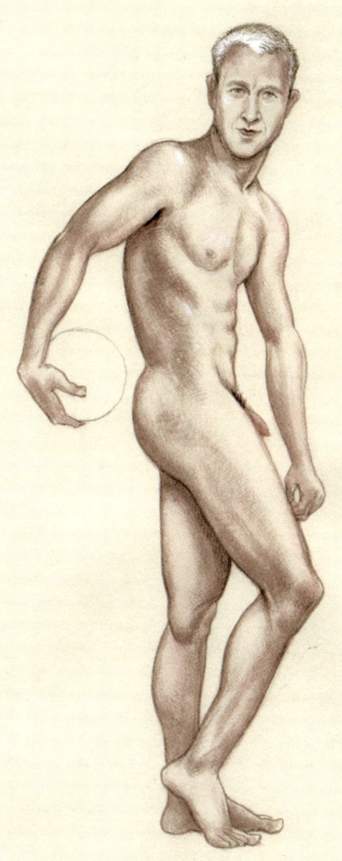

Anderson Cooper

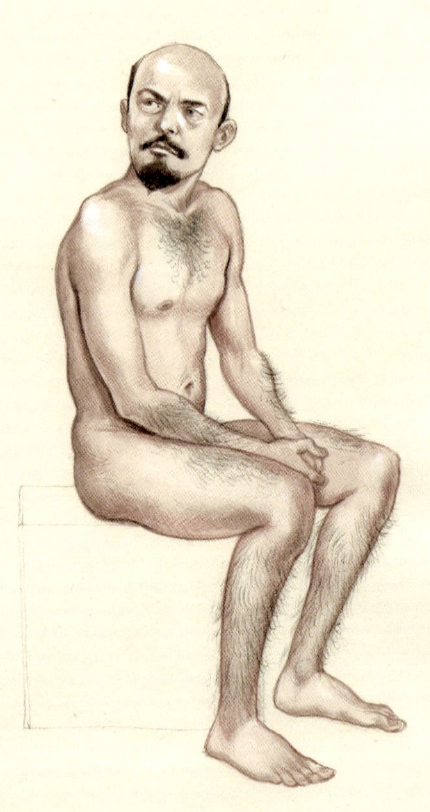

Vladimir Lenin

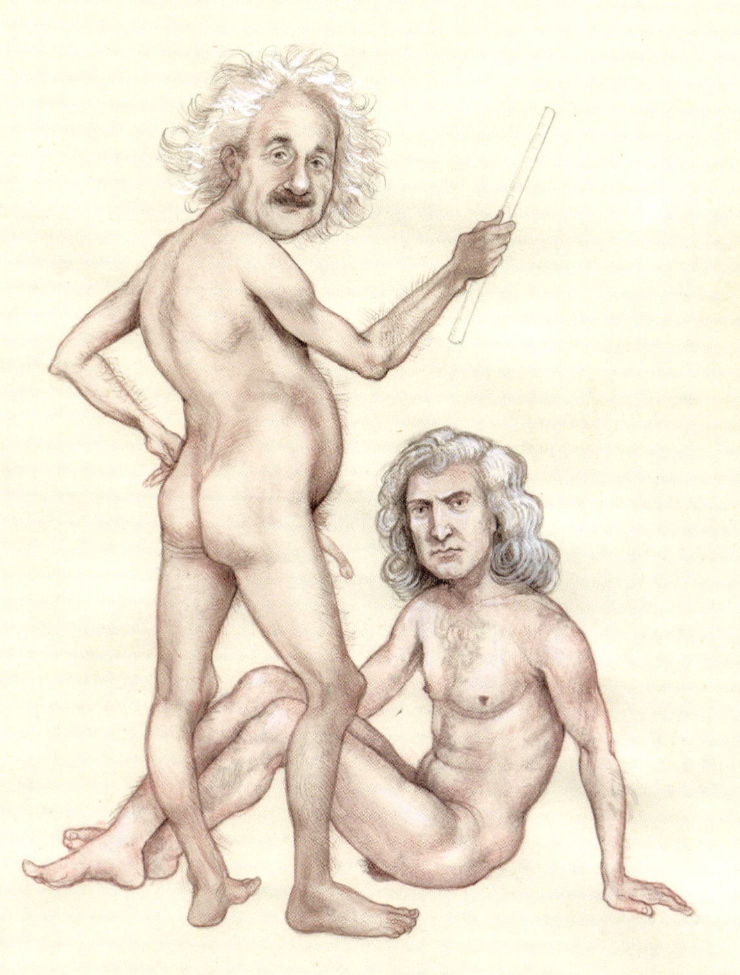

THE SCIENTISTS

Albert Einstein *&* Isaac Newton

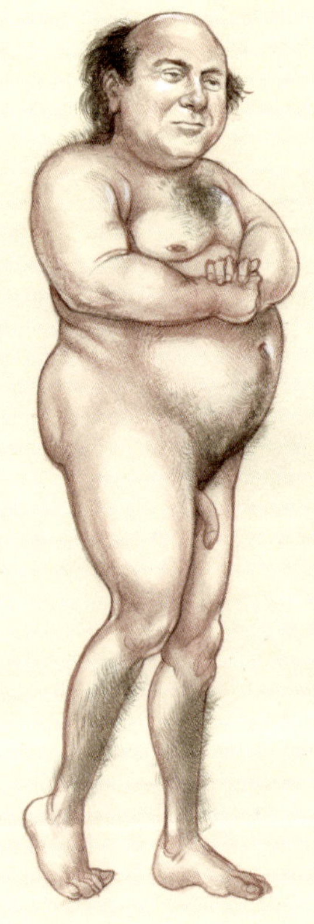

Danny DeVito

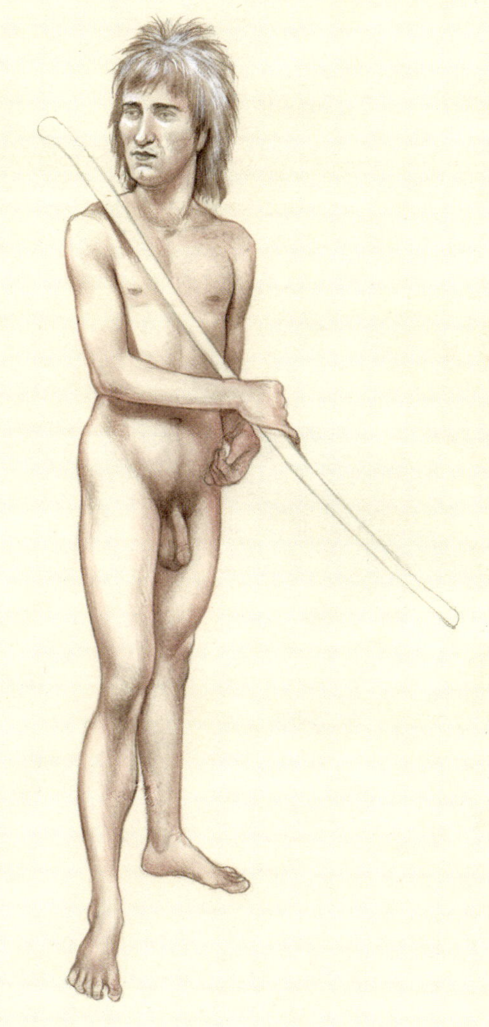

Rod Stewart

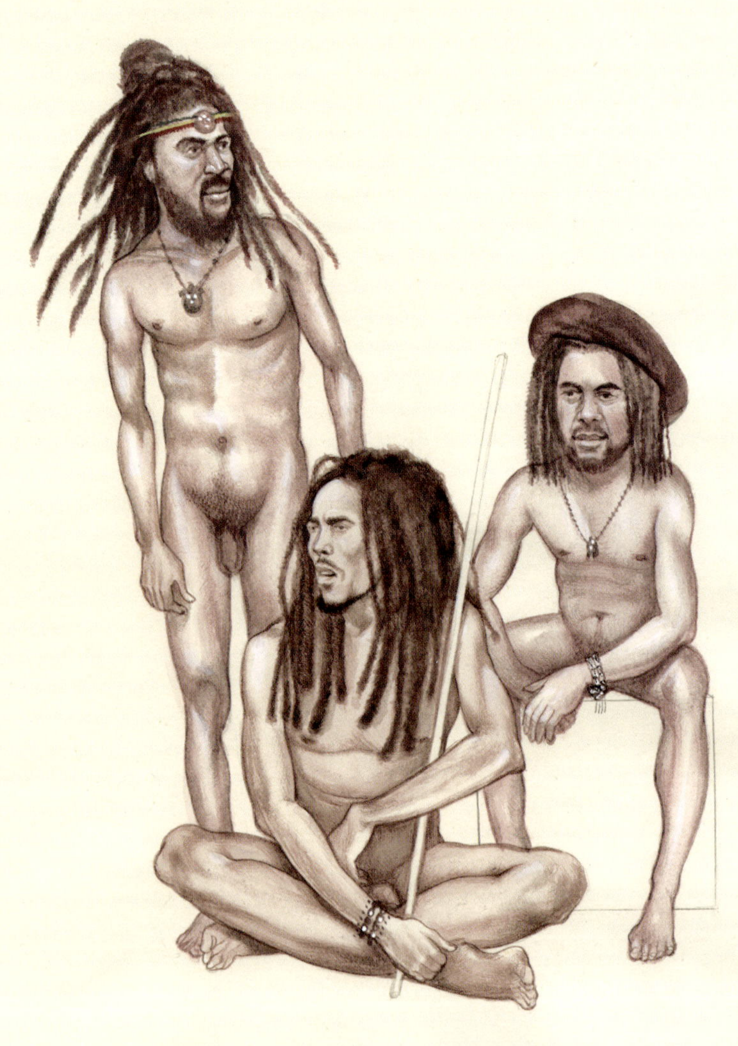

THE REGGAE STARS

Bunny Wailer, Bob Marley & Peter Tosh

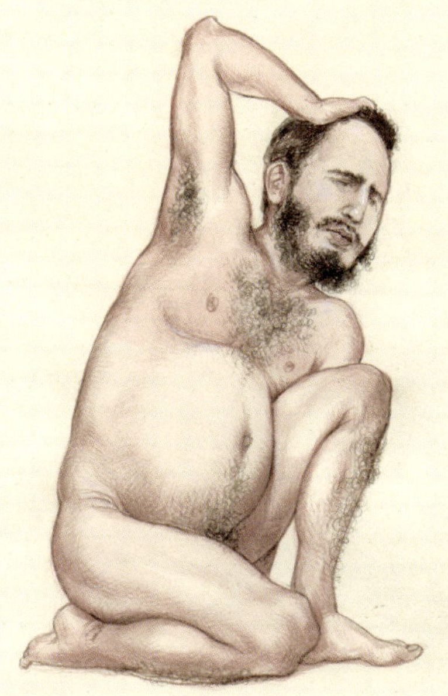

Fidel Castro

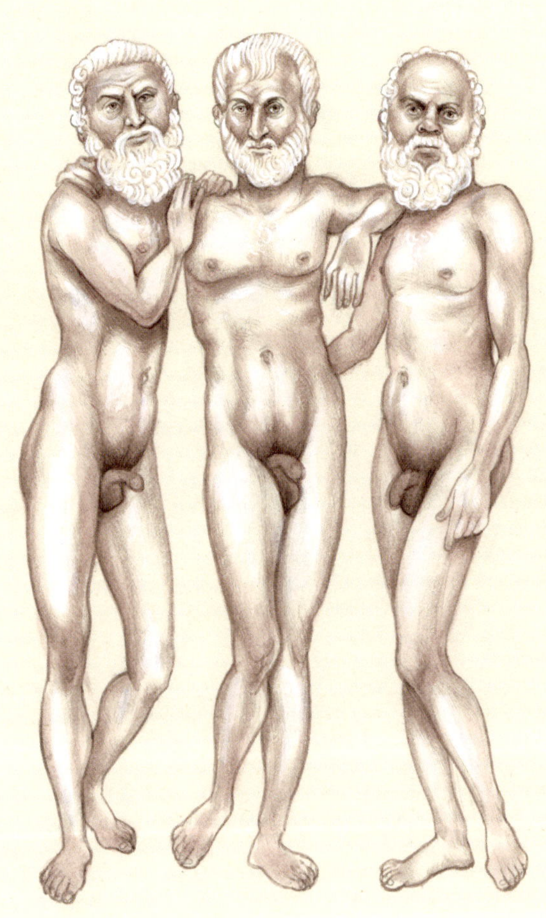

THE THINKERS

Plato, Socrates & Aristotle

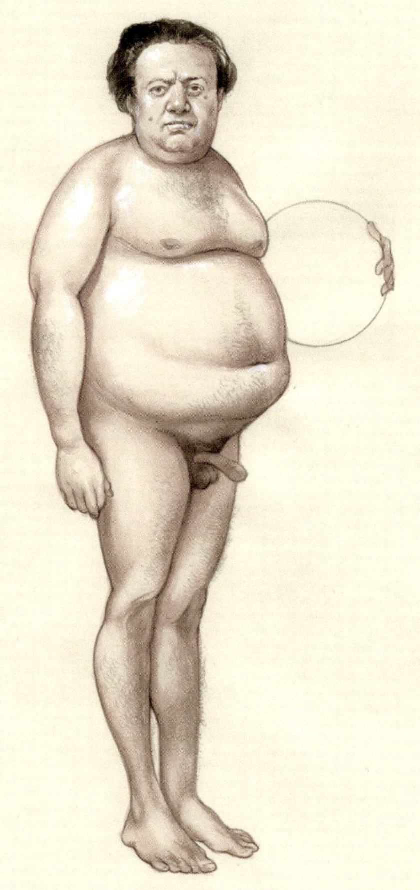

Diego Rivera

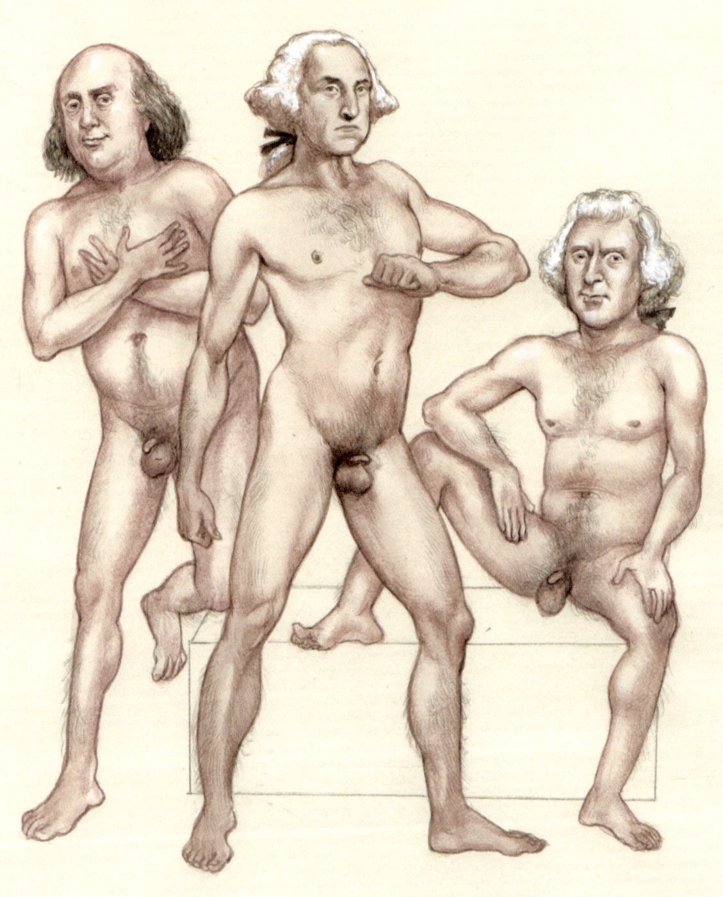

THE FATHERS

Benjamin Franklin, George Washington & Thomas Jefferson

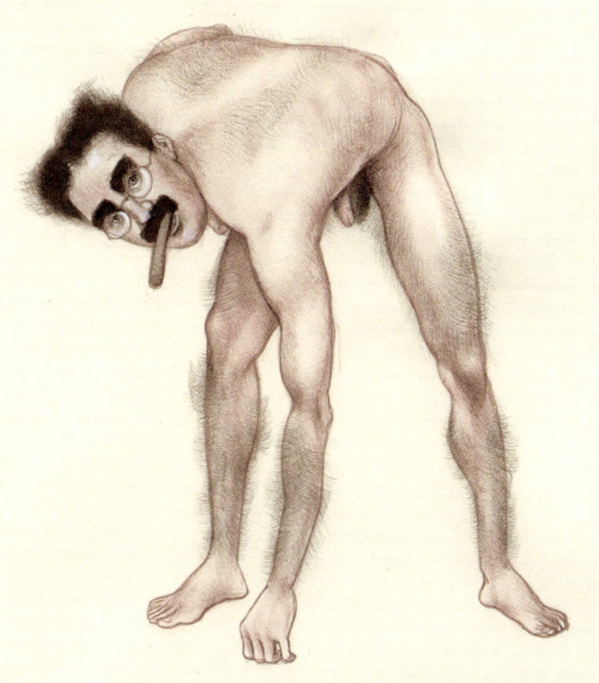

Groucho Marx

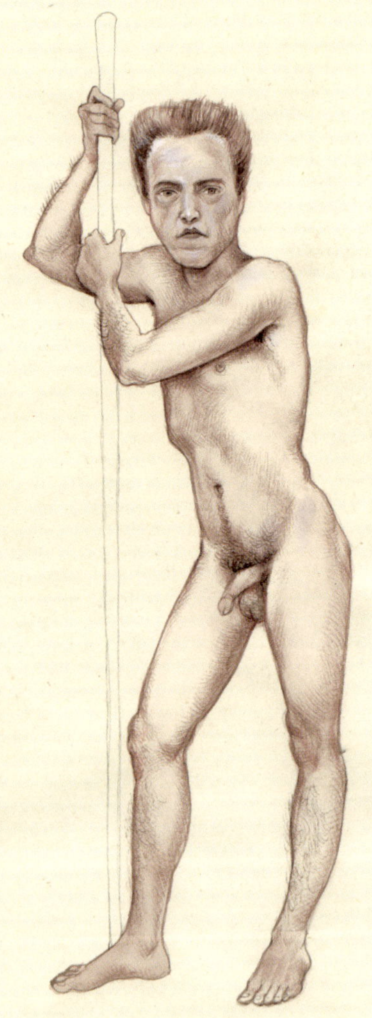

Christopher Walken

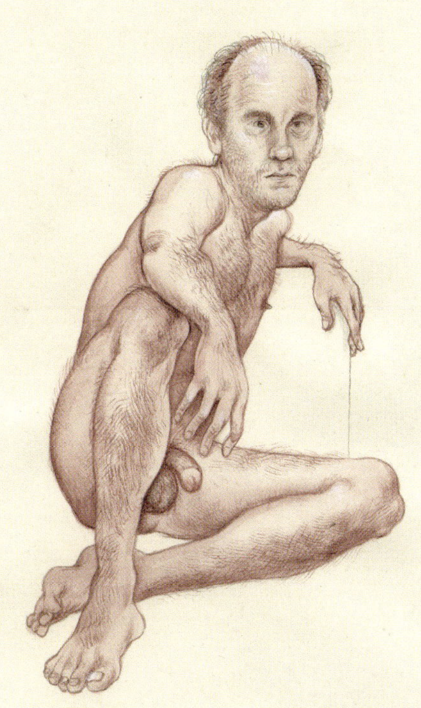

John Malkovich

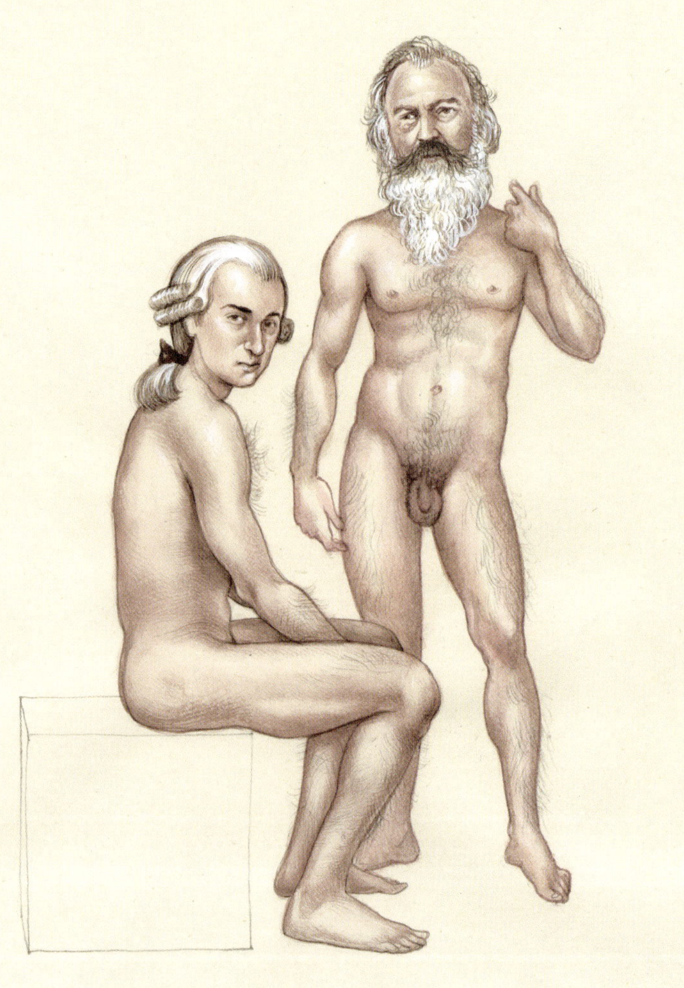

THE COMPOSERS

Mozart & Brahms

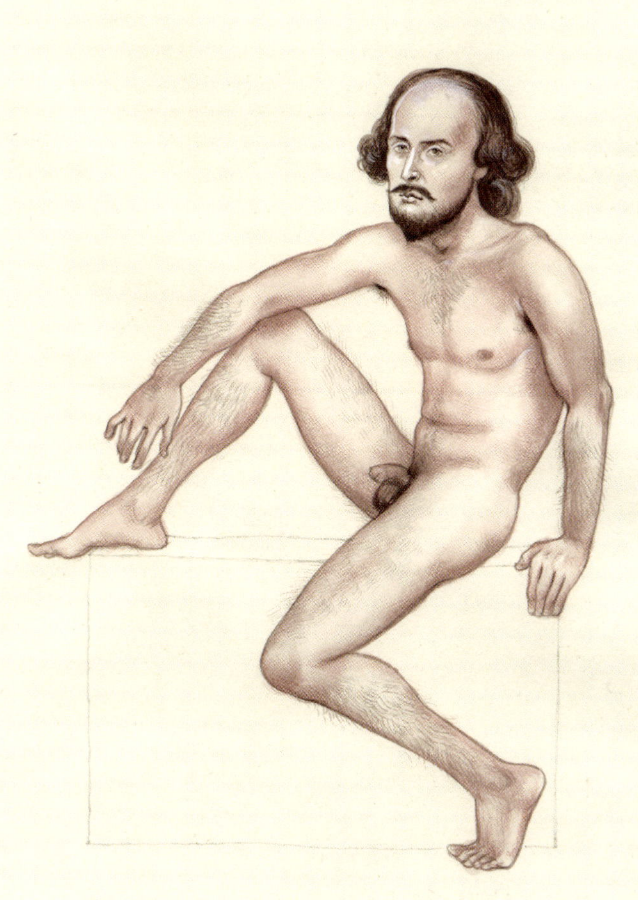

William Shakespeare

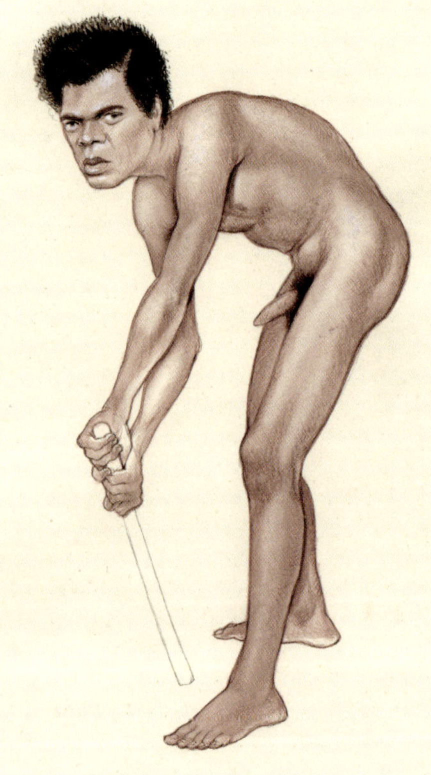

Samuel L. Jackson

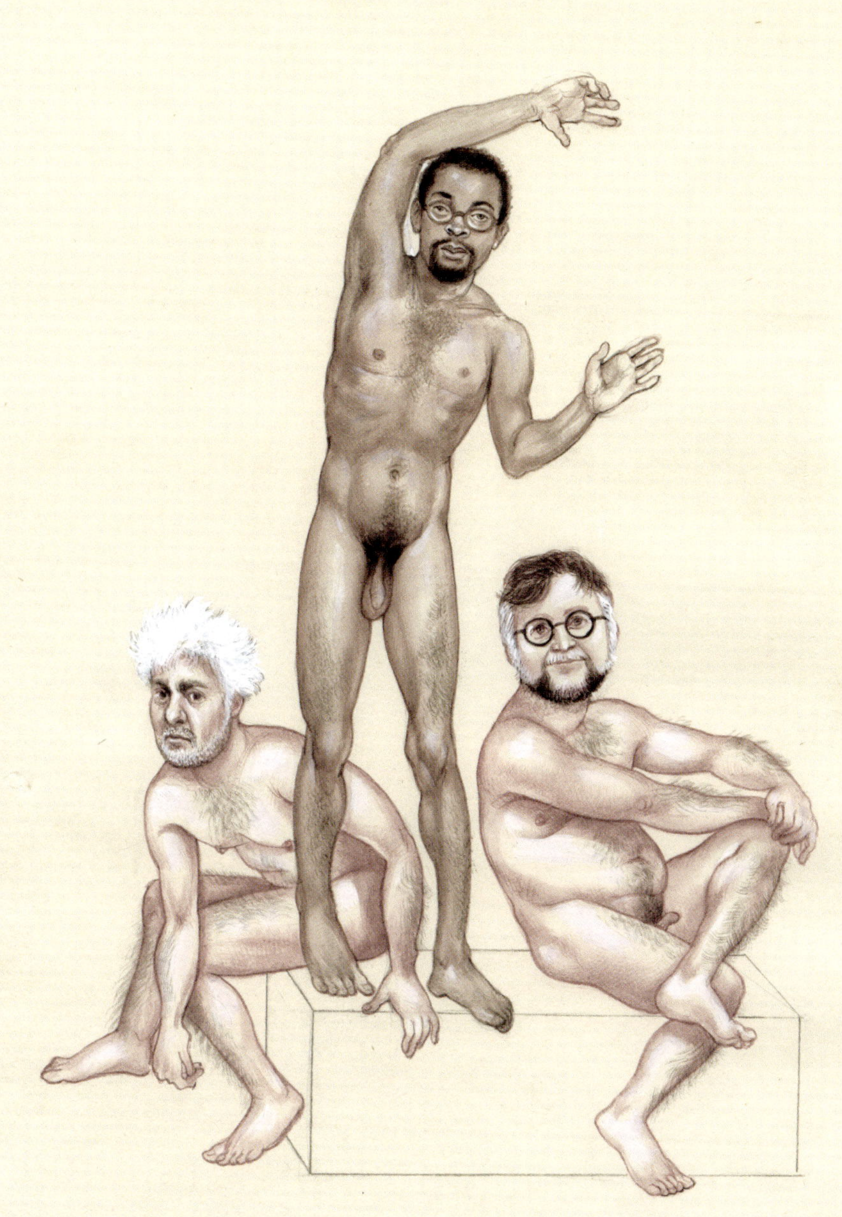

THE DIRECTORS

Pedro Almodóvar, Spike Lee & Guillermo del Toro

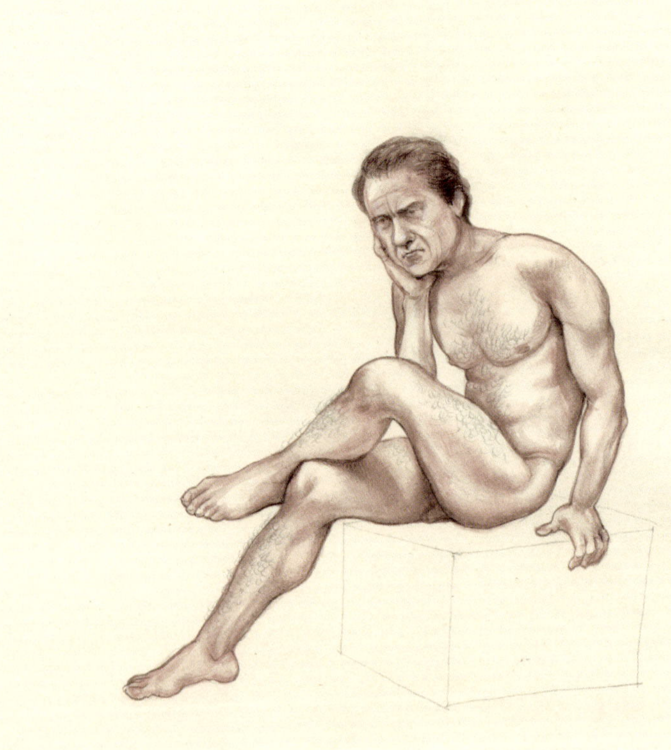

Harvey Keitel

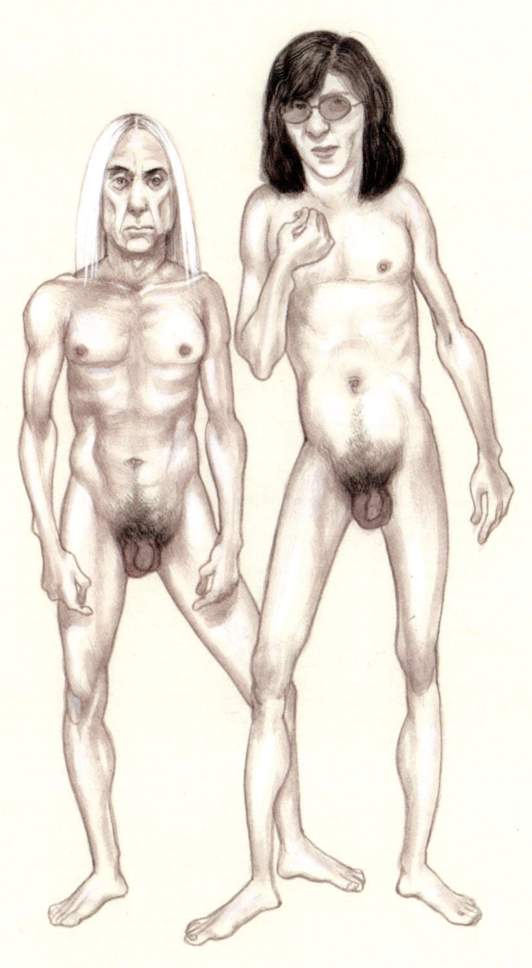

THE PUNKS

Iggy Pop & Joey Ramone

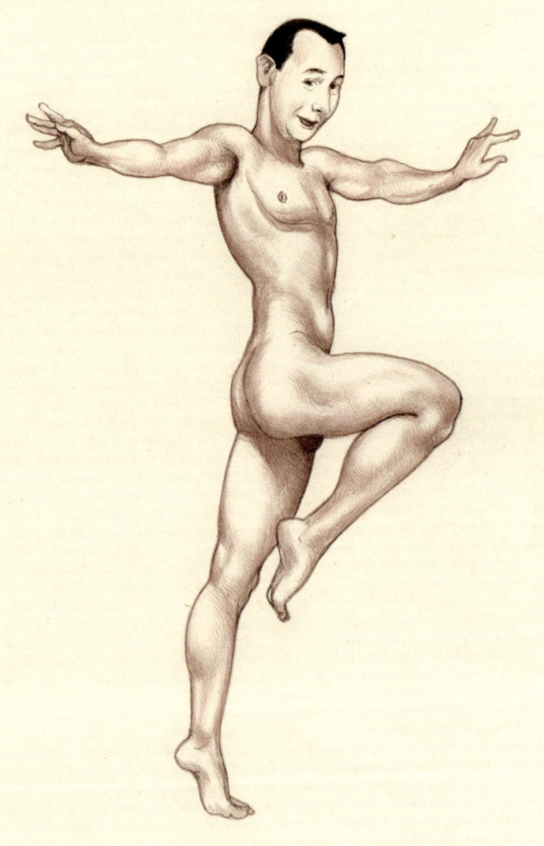

Pee-wee Herman

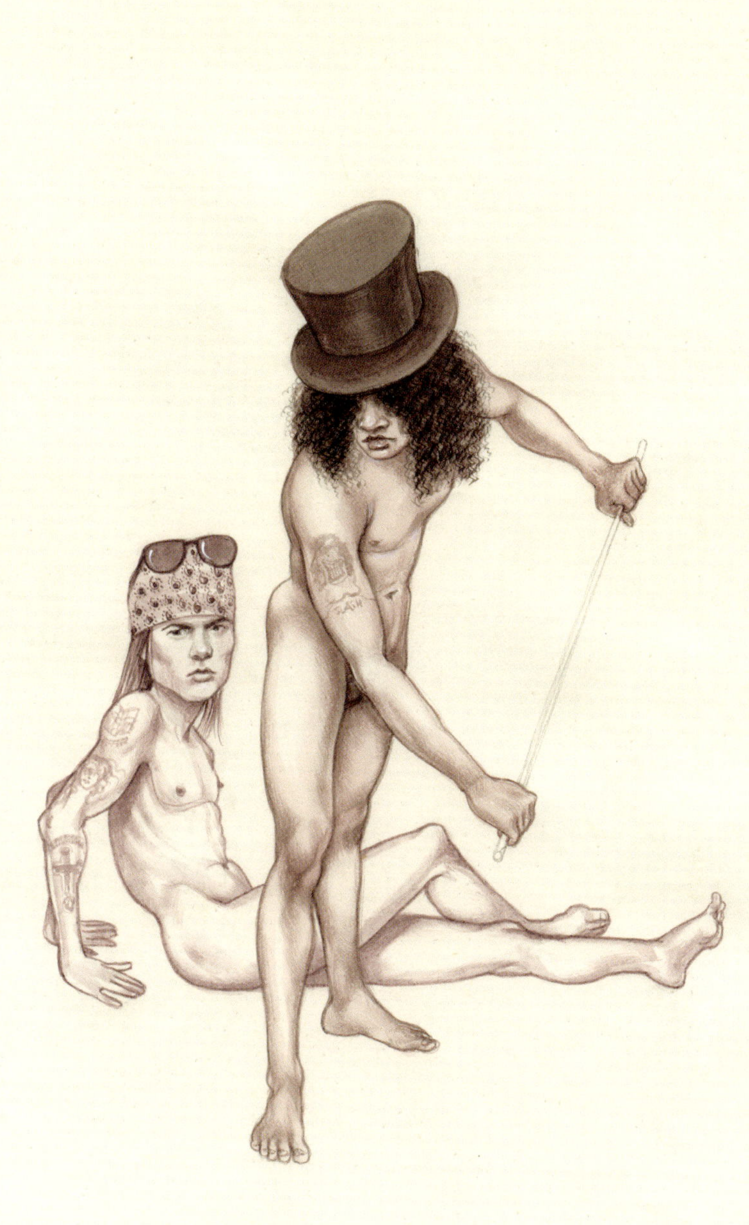

THE ROCK STARS

Axl Rose & Slash

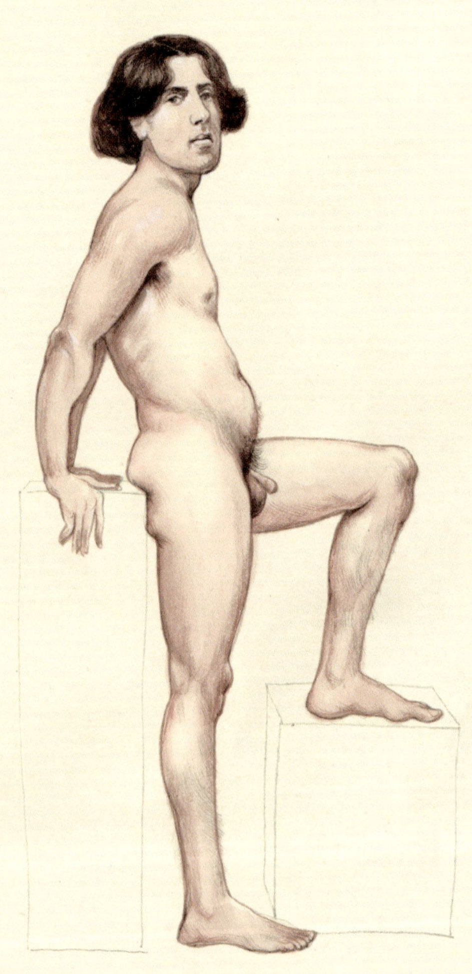

Oscar Wilde

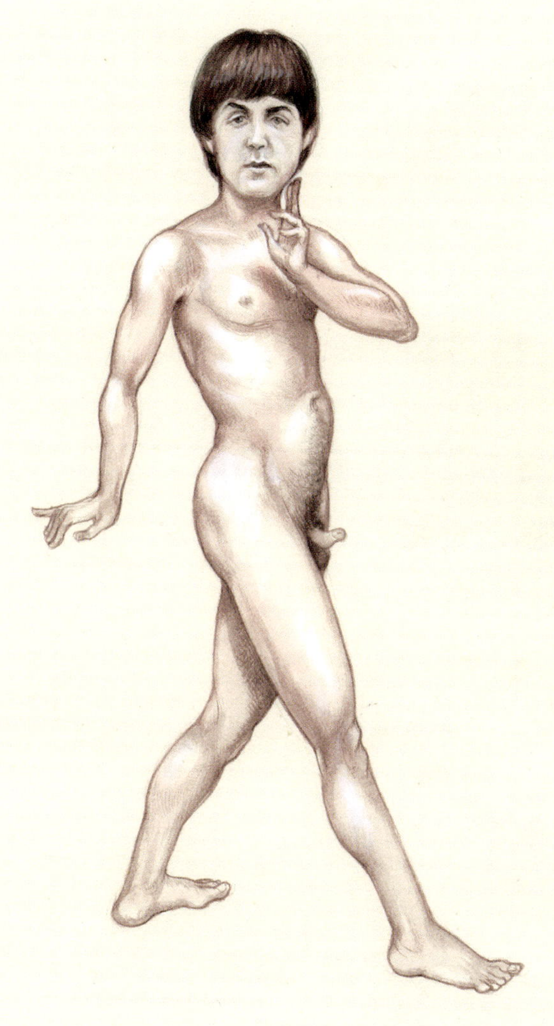

Paul McCartney

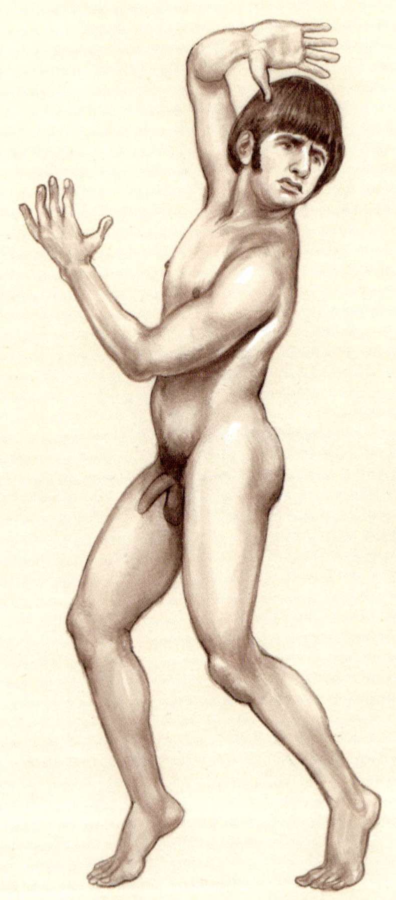

Ringo Starr

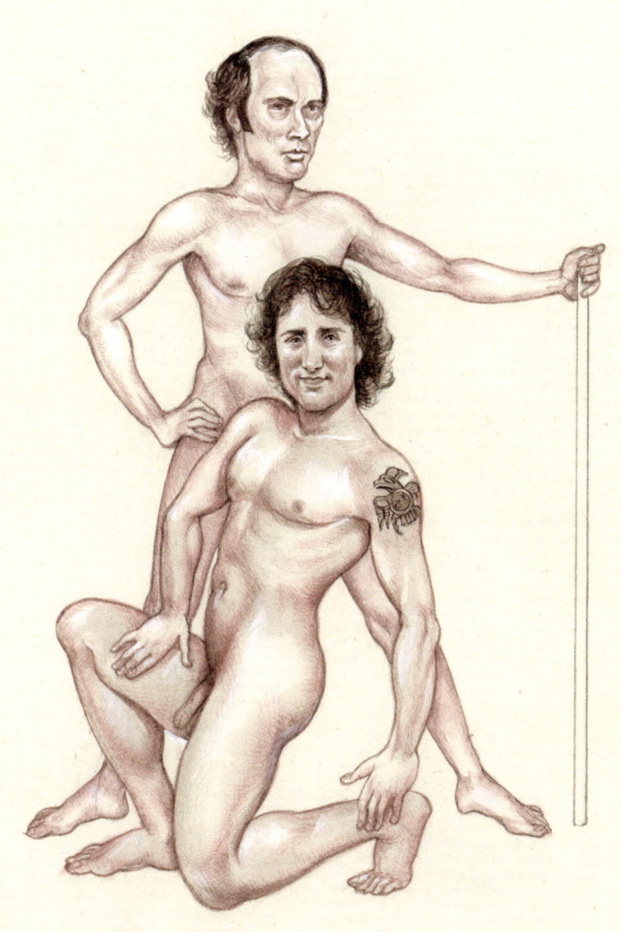

THE CANADIANS

Pierre Elliot Trudeau & Justin Trudeau

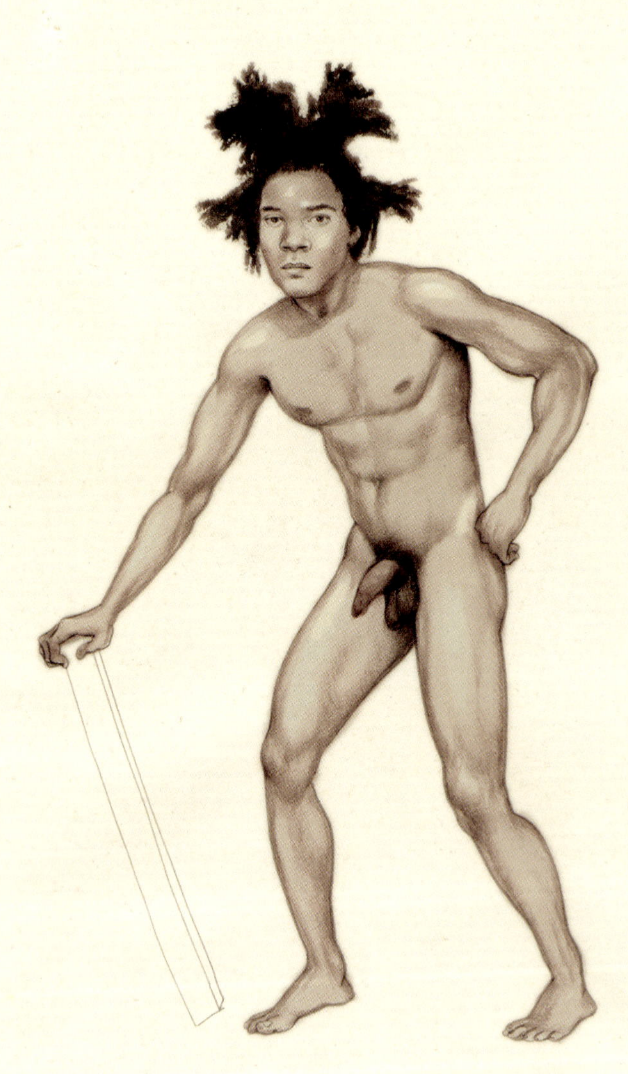

Jean-Michel Basquiat

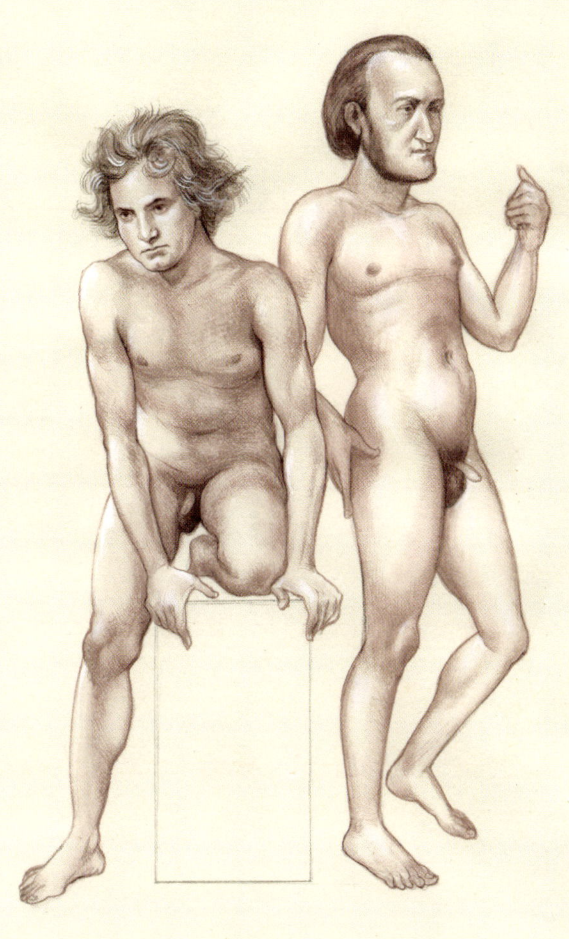

THE CLASSICAL MASTERS

Beethoven & Wagner

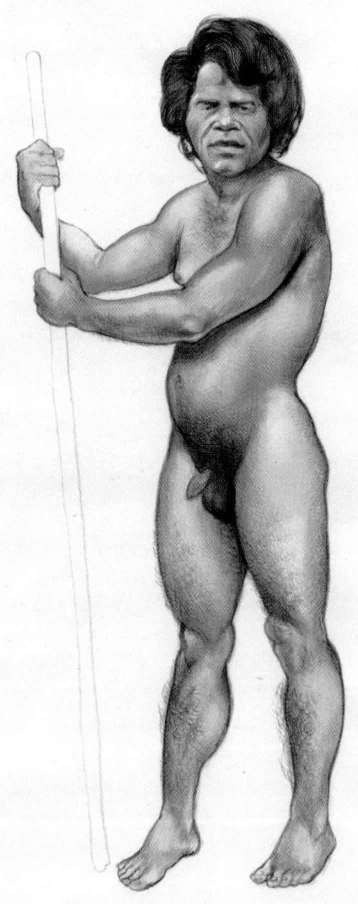

James Brown

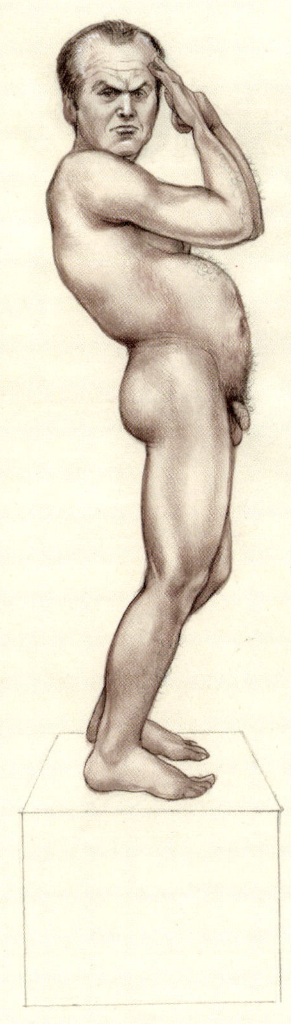

Jack Nicholson

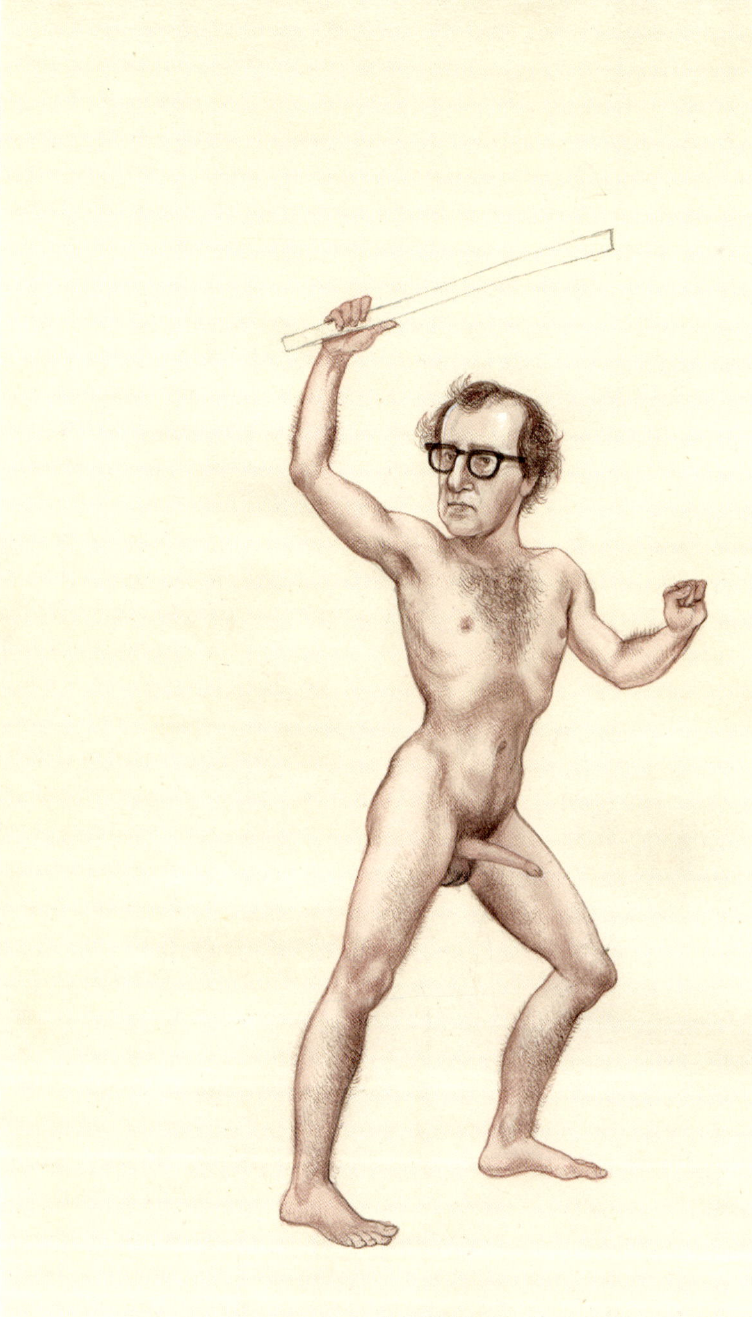

Woody Allen

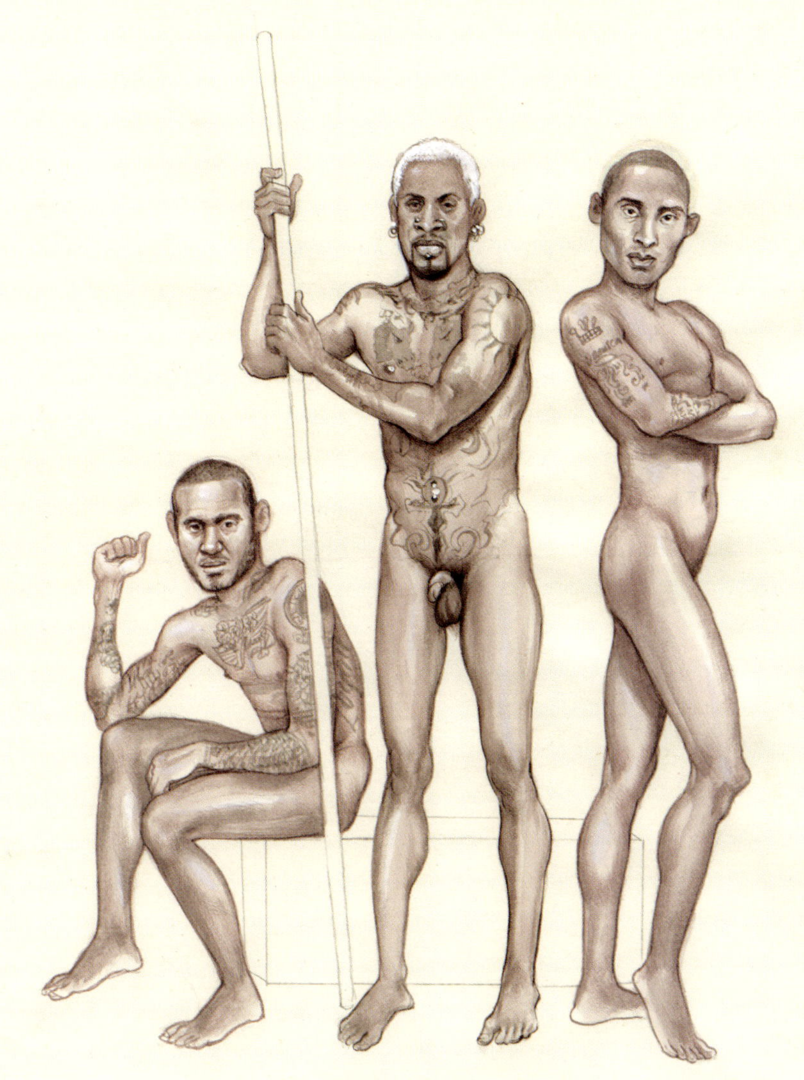

THE BASKETBALL STARS

LeBron James, Dennis Rodman & Kobe Bryant

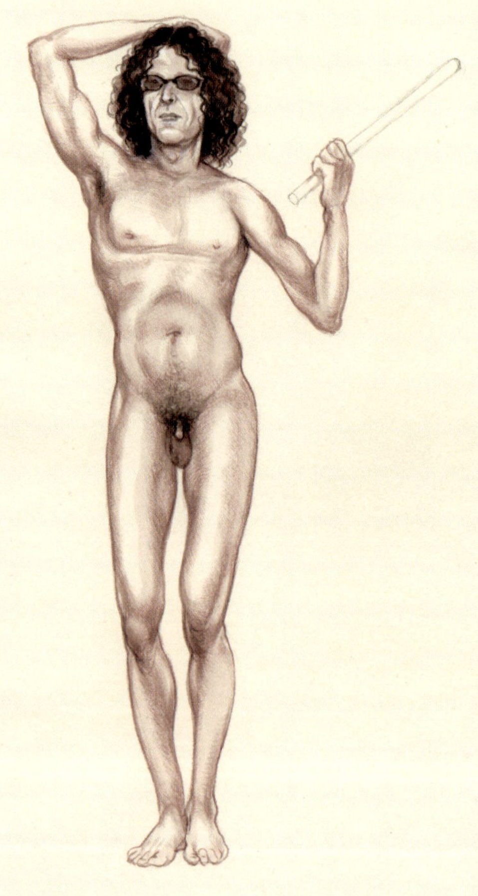

Howard Stern

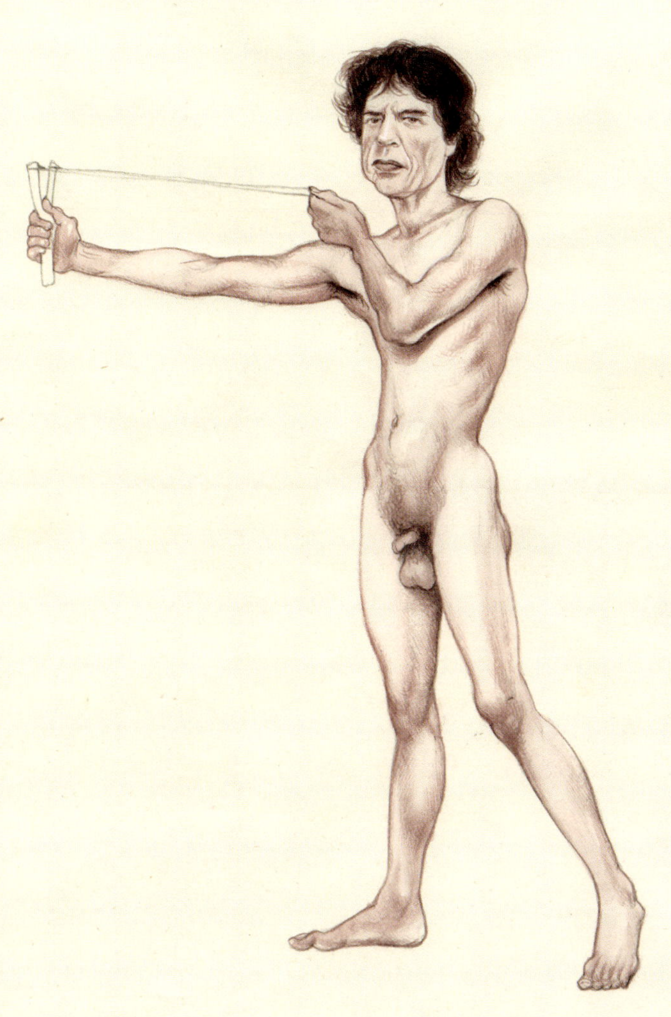

Mick Jagger

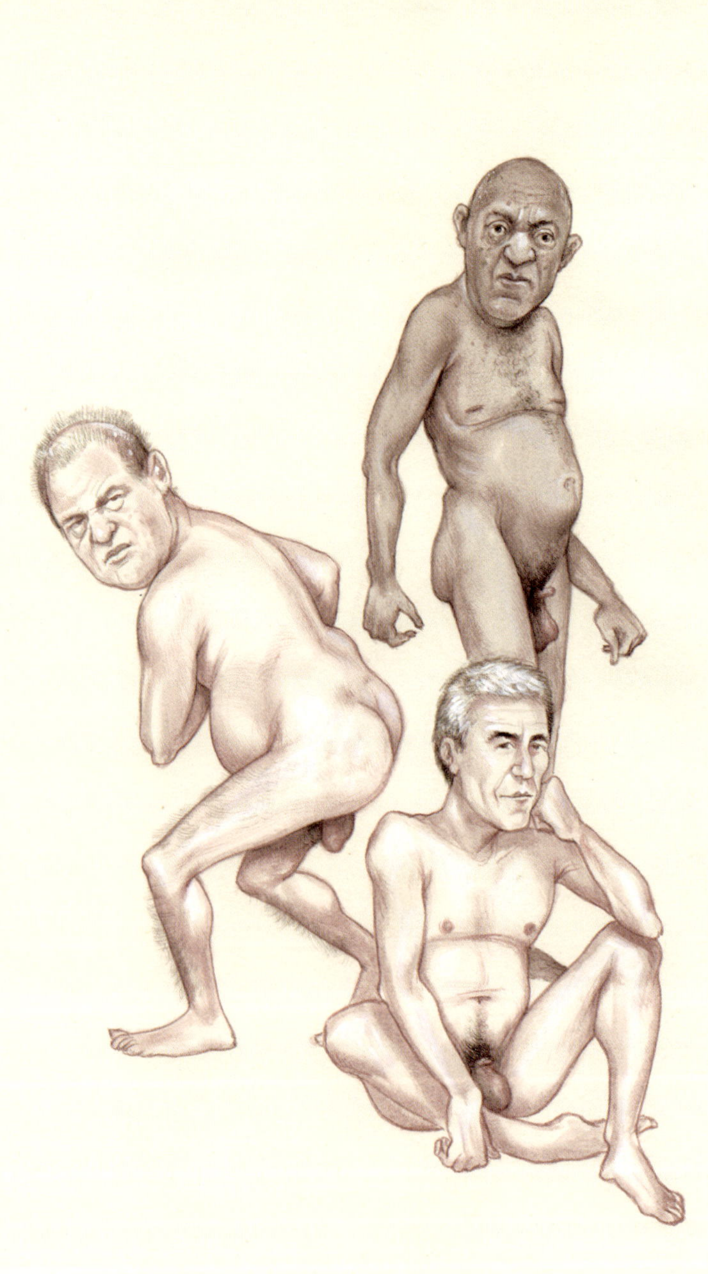

THE RAPISTS

Weinstein, Cosby & Epstein

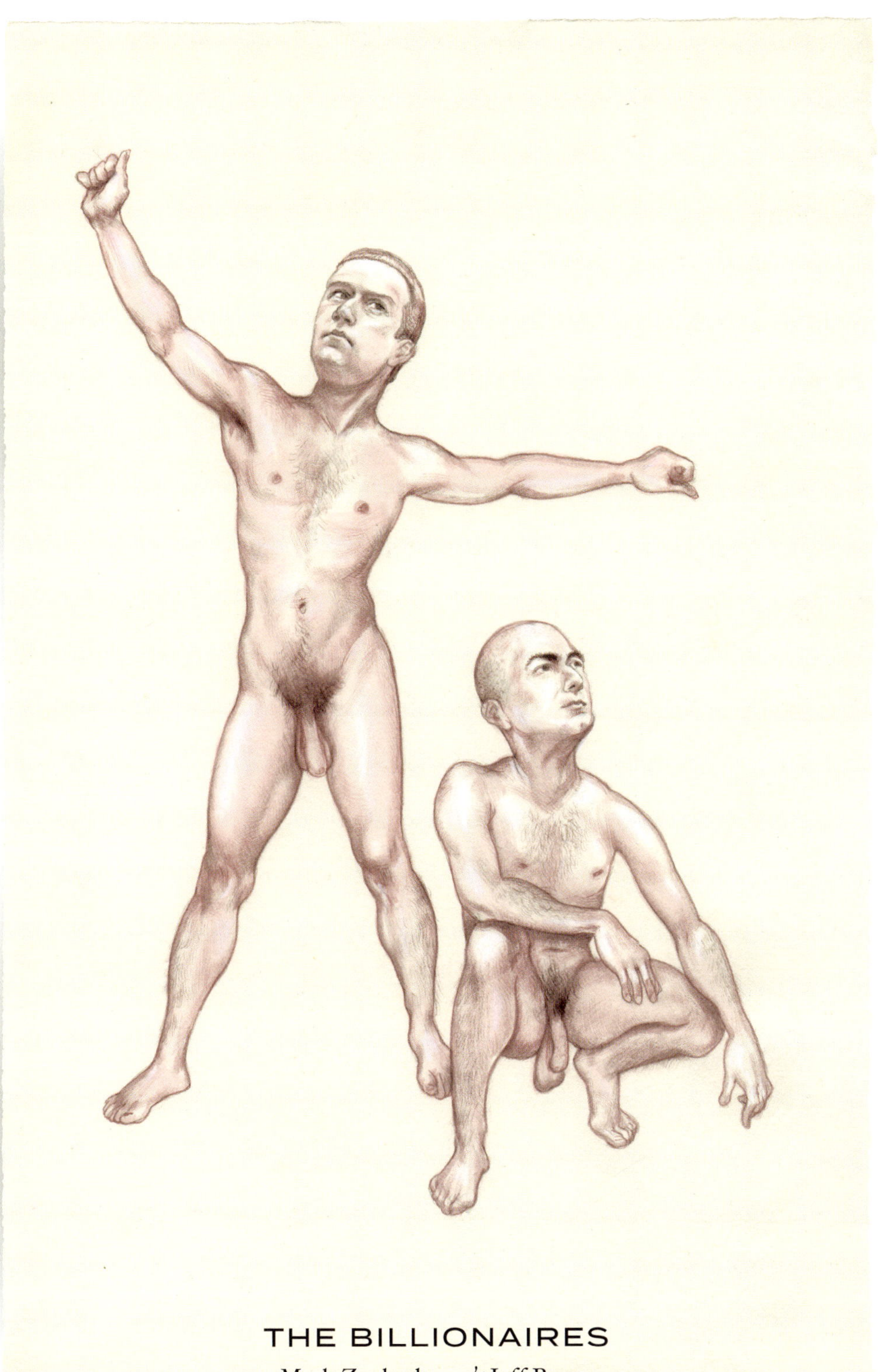

THE BILLIONAIRES

Mark Zuckerberg & Jeff Bezos

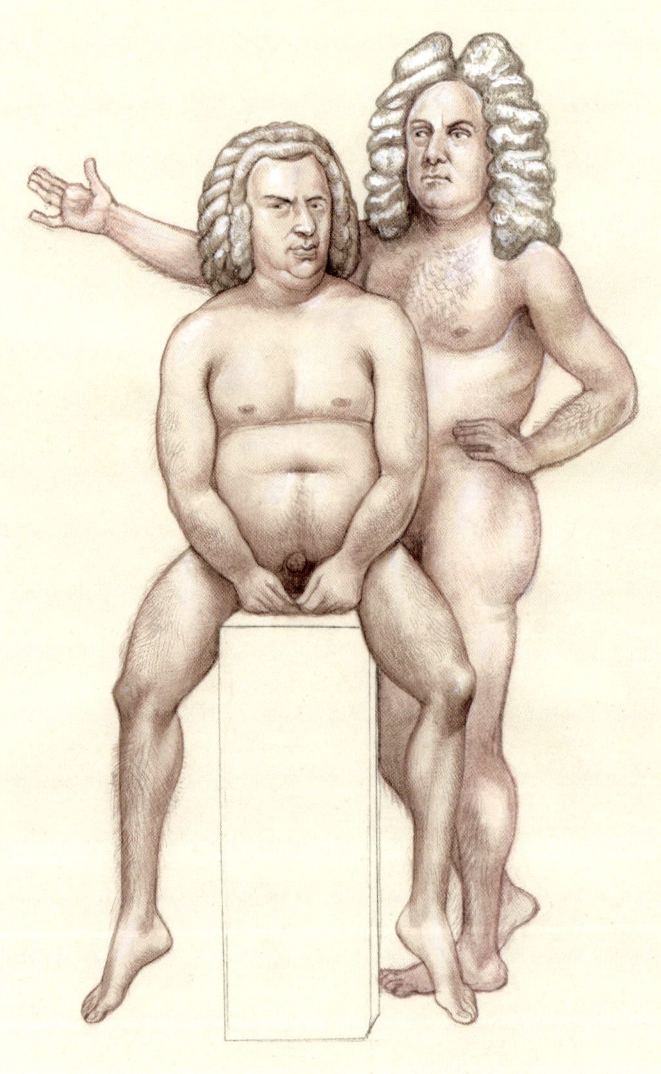

THE BAROQUE MASTERS

Bach & Handel

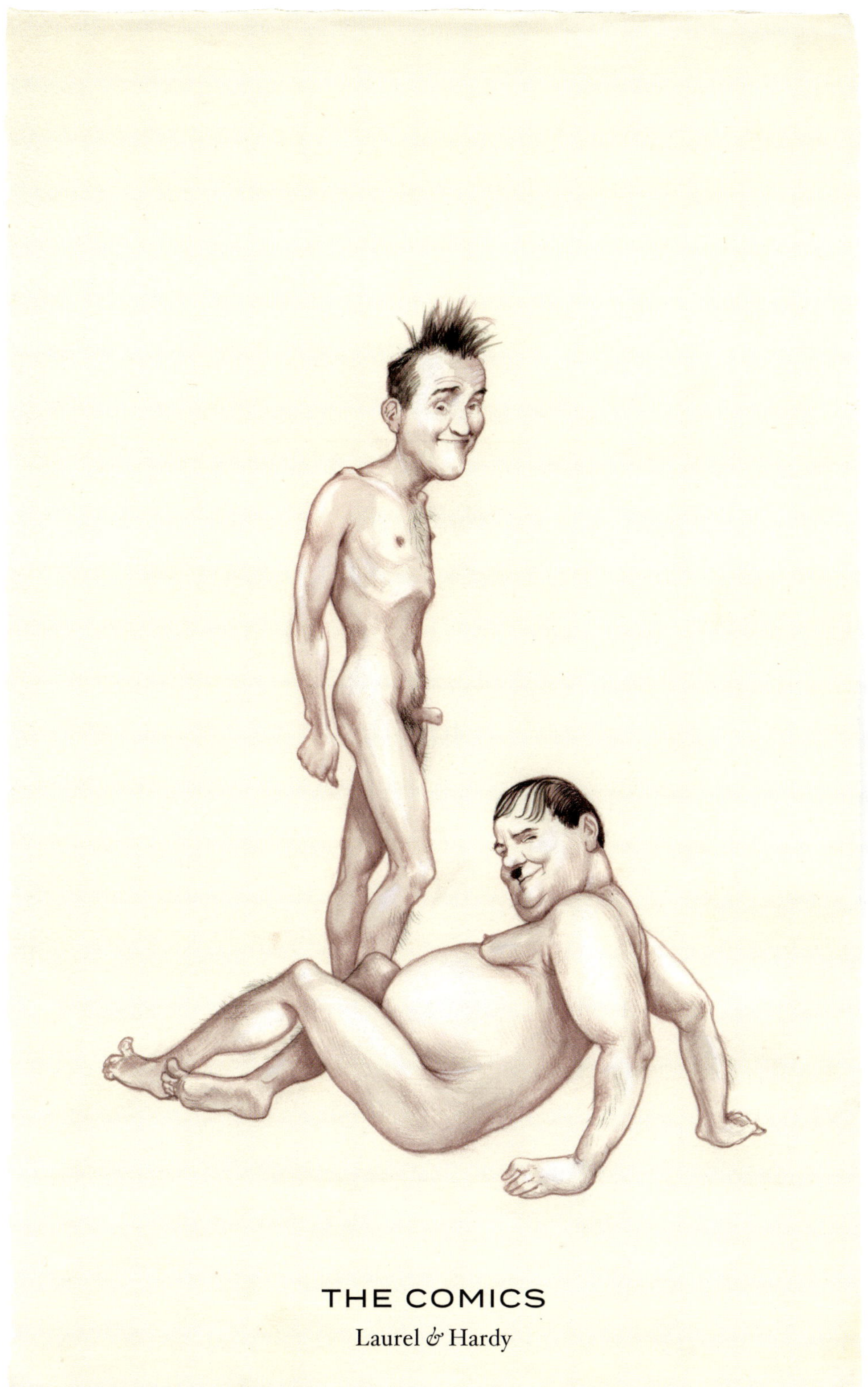

THE COMICS

Laurel & Hardy

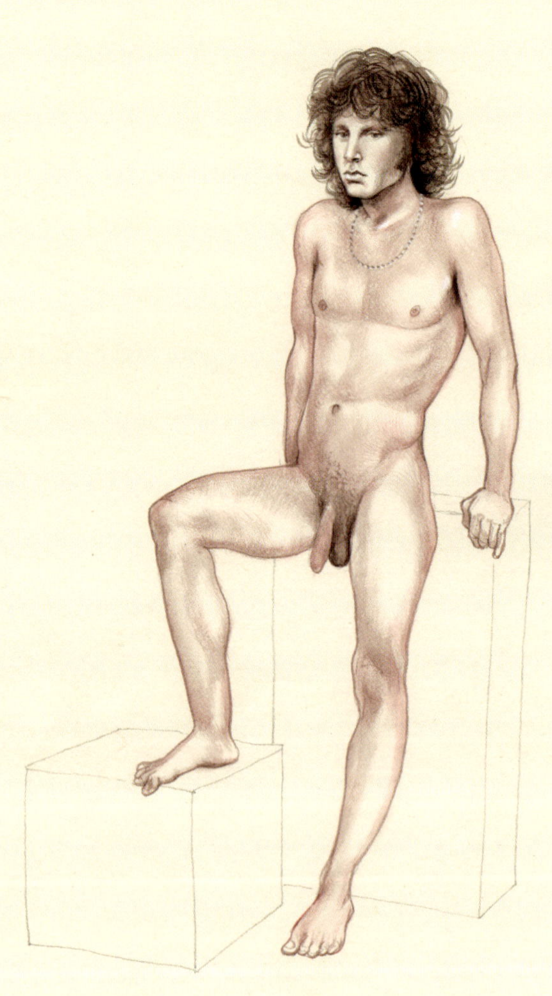

Jim Morrison

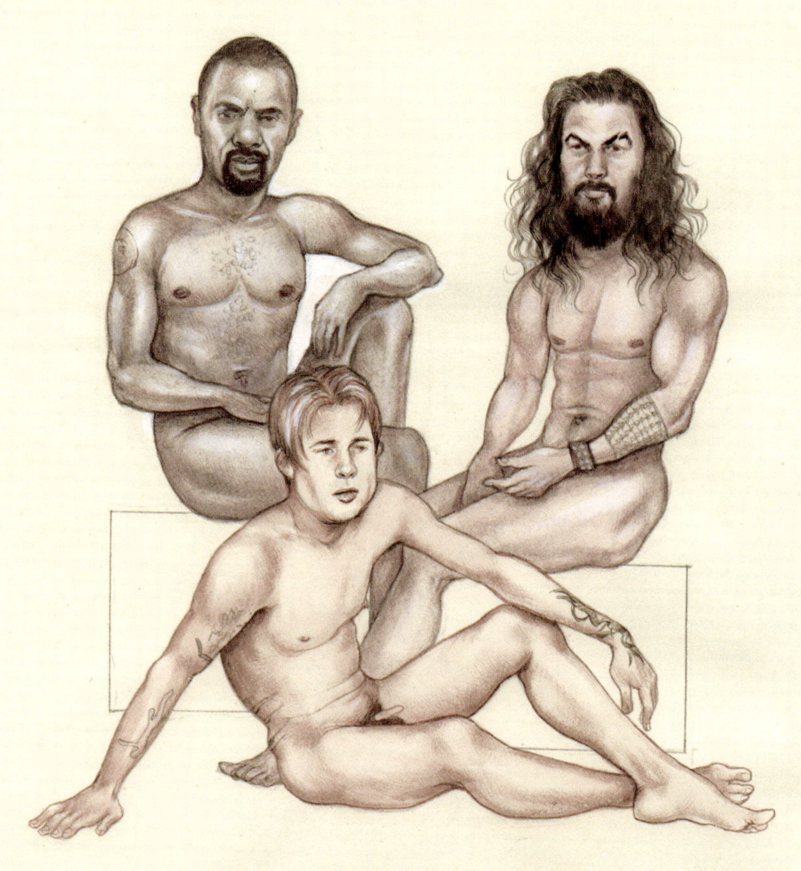

THE HUNKS

Idris Elba, Brad Pitt & Jason Momoa

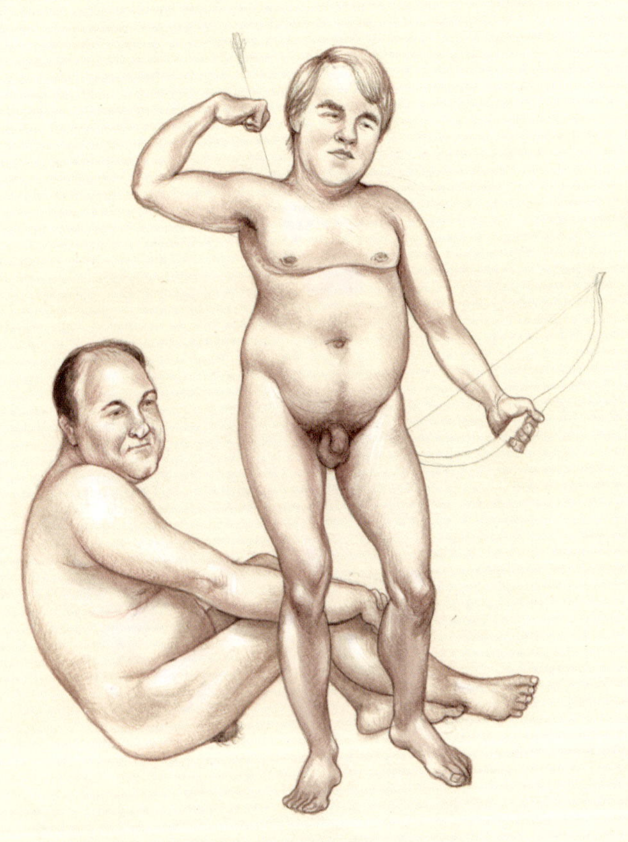

THE DEARLY DEPARTED

James Gandolfini & Philip Seymour Hoffman

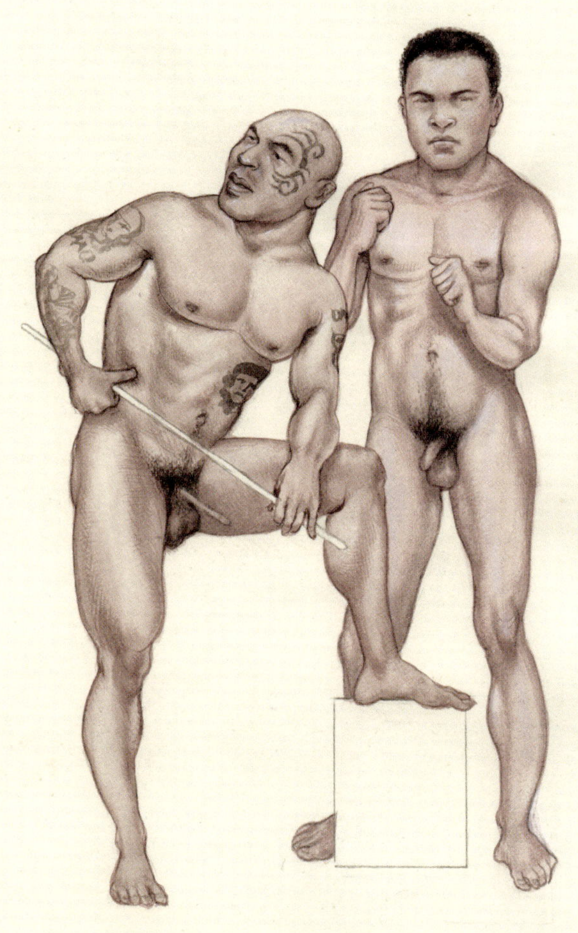

THE FIGHTERS

Mike Tyson & Muhammad Ali

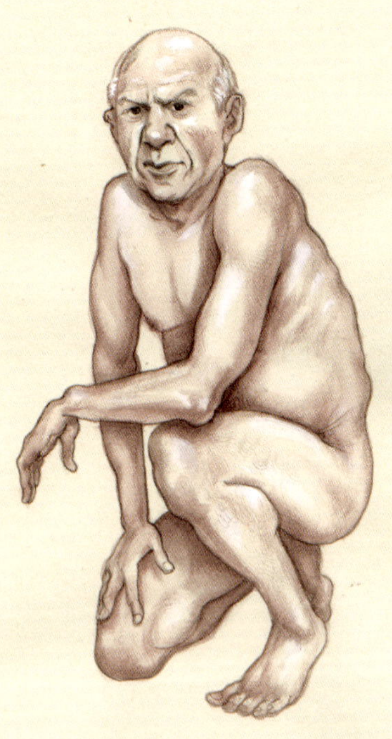

Pablo Picasso

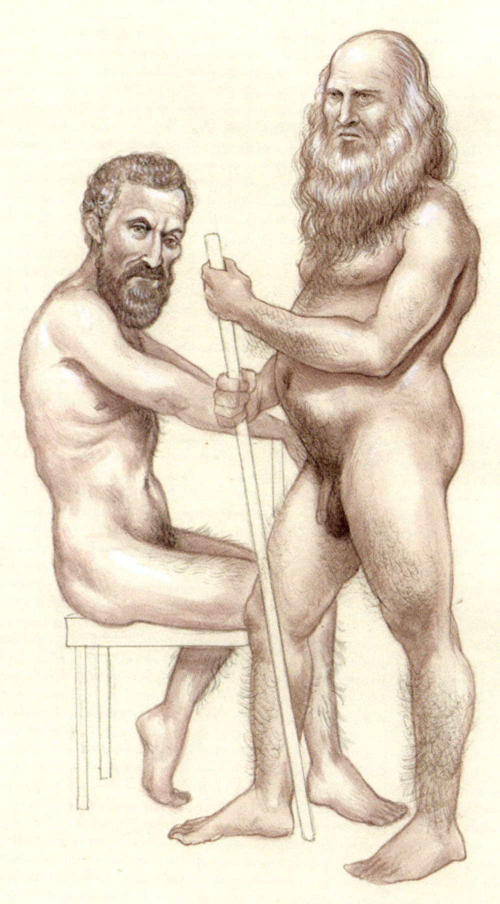

THE GENIUSES

Michelangelo & Leonardo da Vinci

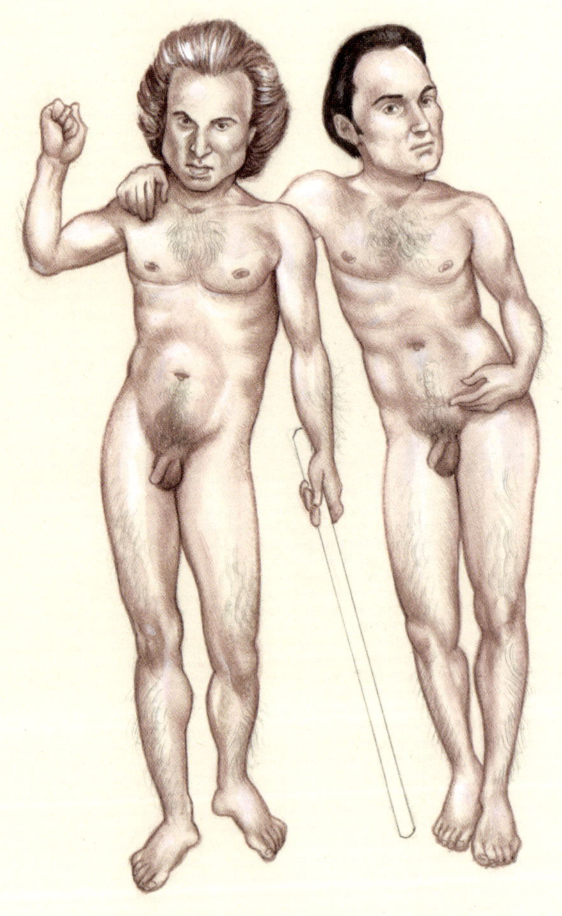

THE LION TAMERS

Siegfried & Roy

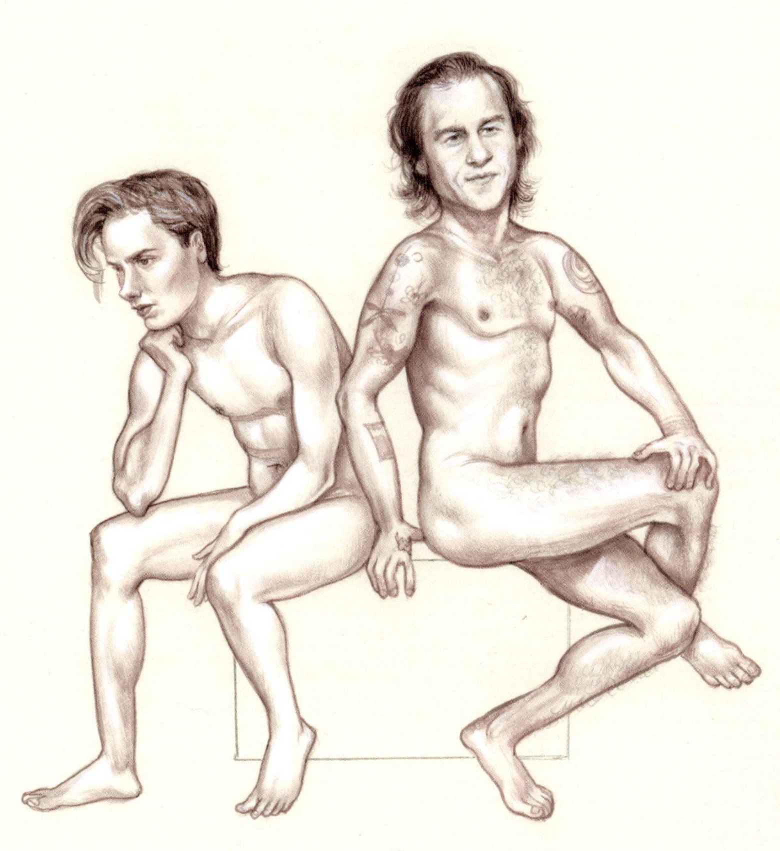

THE HEARTBREAKERS

River Phoenix & Heath Ledger

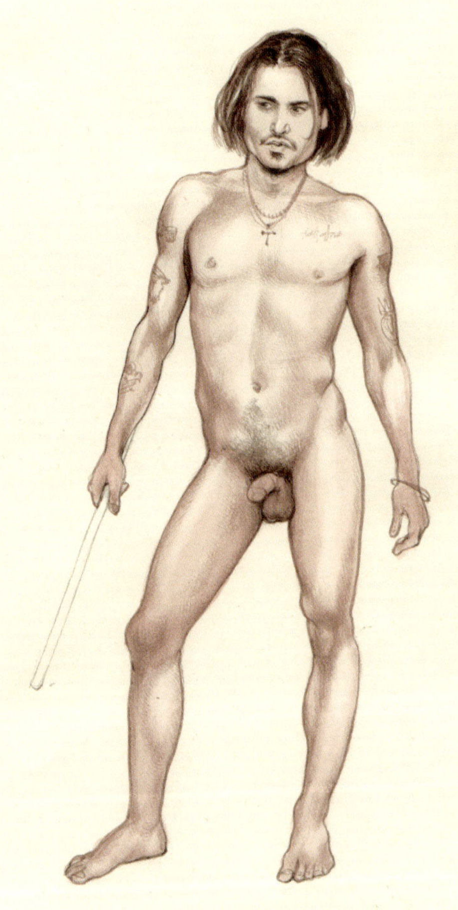

Johnny Depp

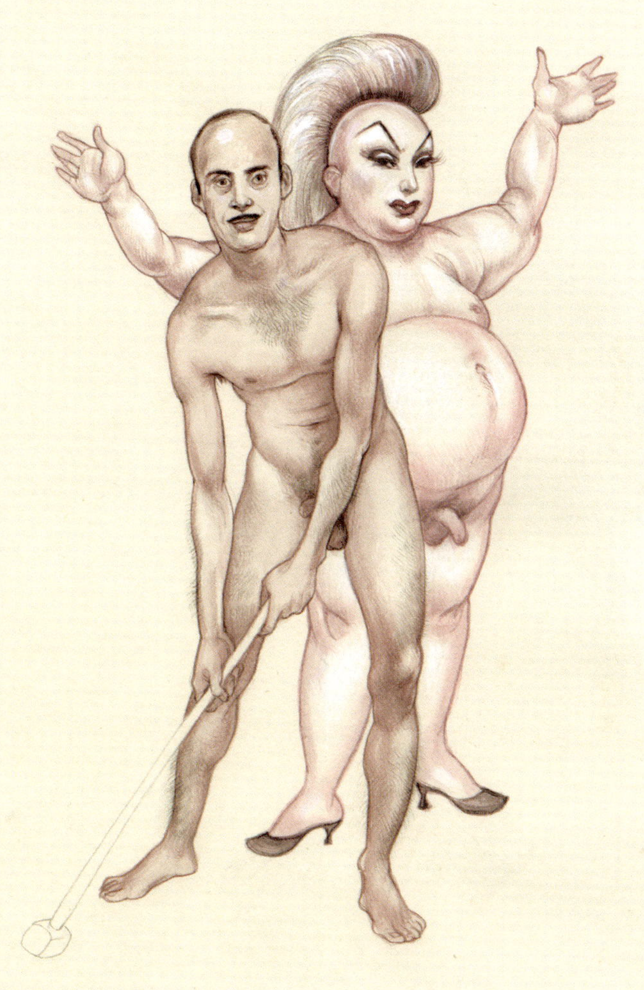

THE OUTRAGEOUS

John Waters & Divine

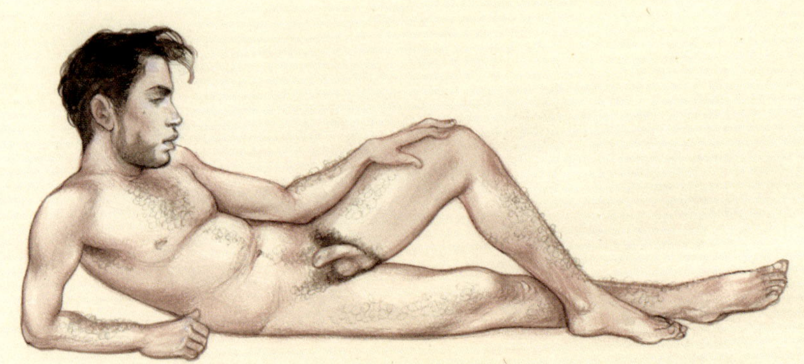

Prince

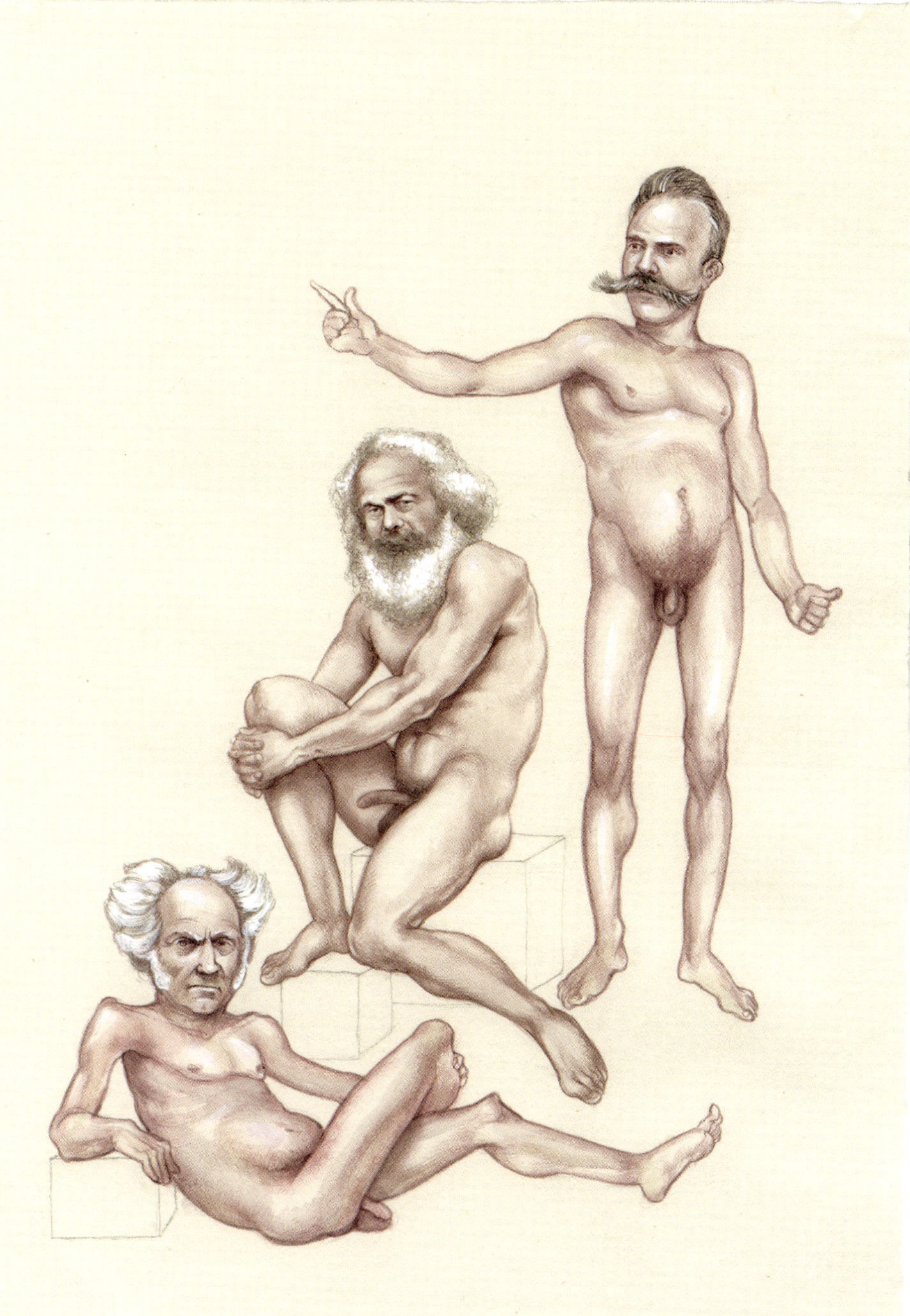

THE PHILOSOPHERS

Schopenhauer, Nietzsche & Marx

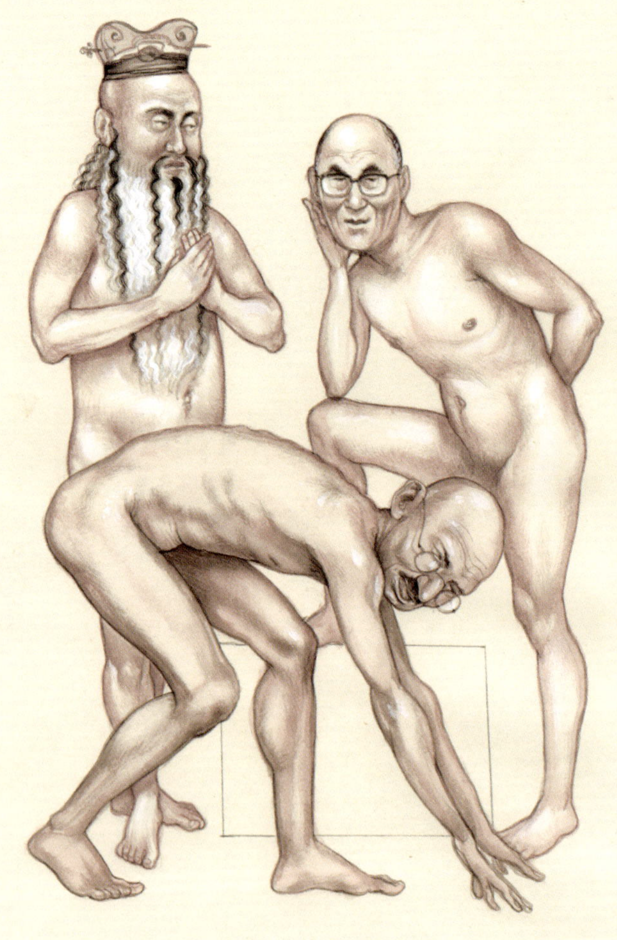

THE SPIRITUAL LEADERS

Confucius, Gandhi & the 14th Dalai Lama

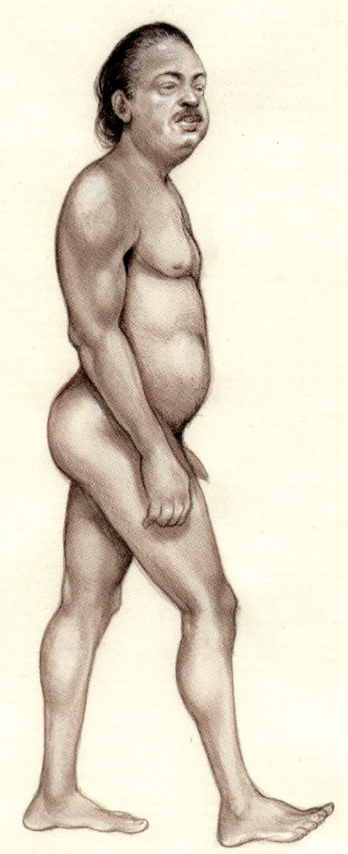

Al Sharpton

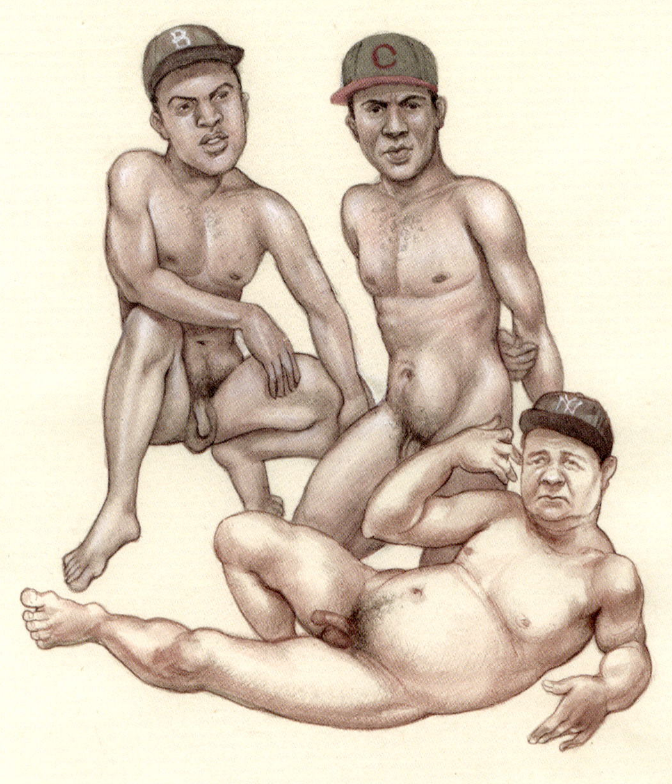

THE BASEBALL PLAYERS

Jackie Robinson, Babe Ruth & Satchel Paige

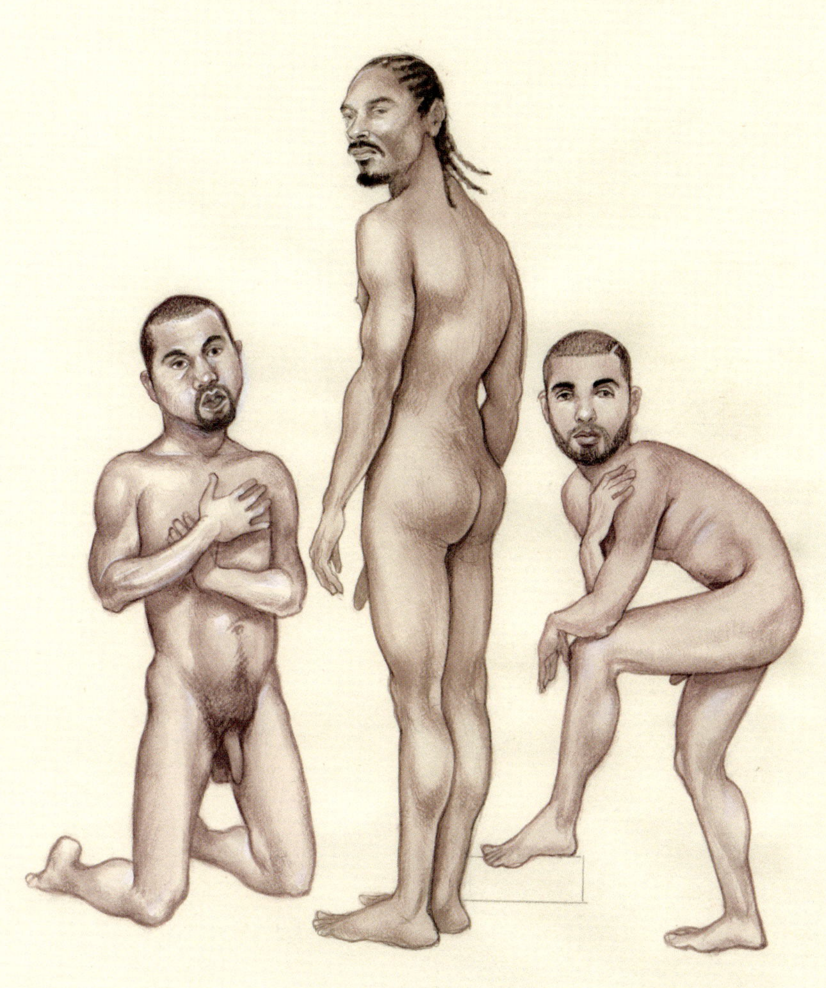

THE RAPPERS

Kanye West, Snoop Dogg & Drake

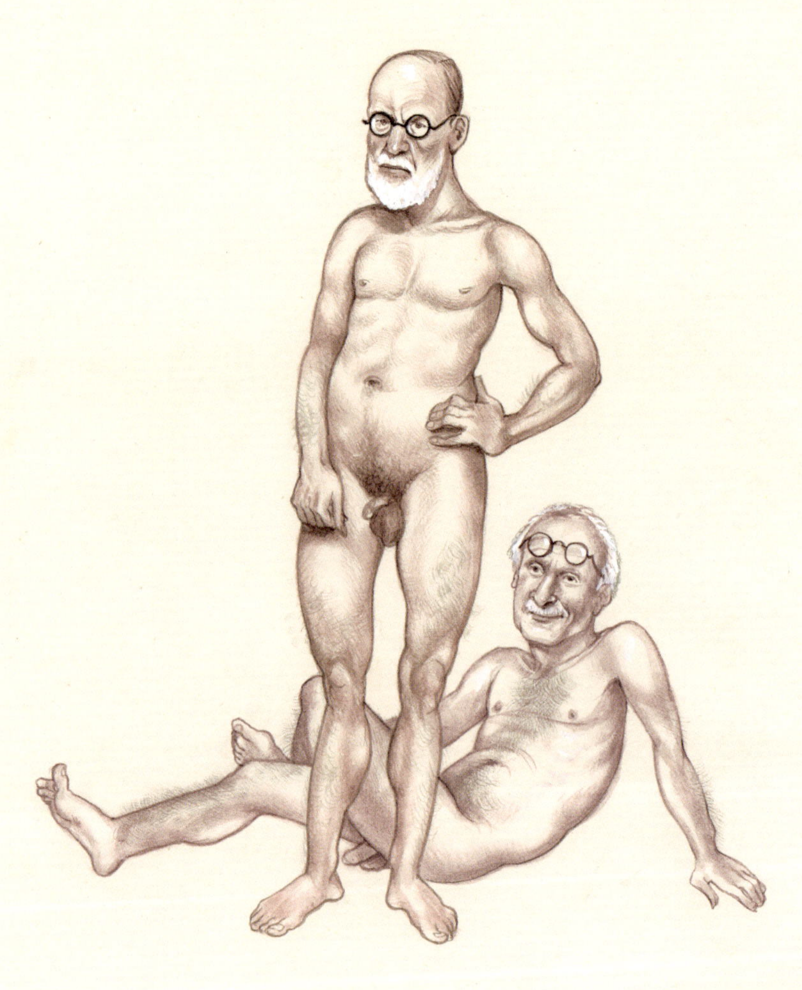

THE THERAPISTS

Sigmund Freud & Carl Jung

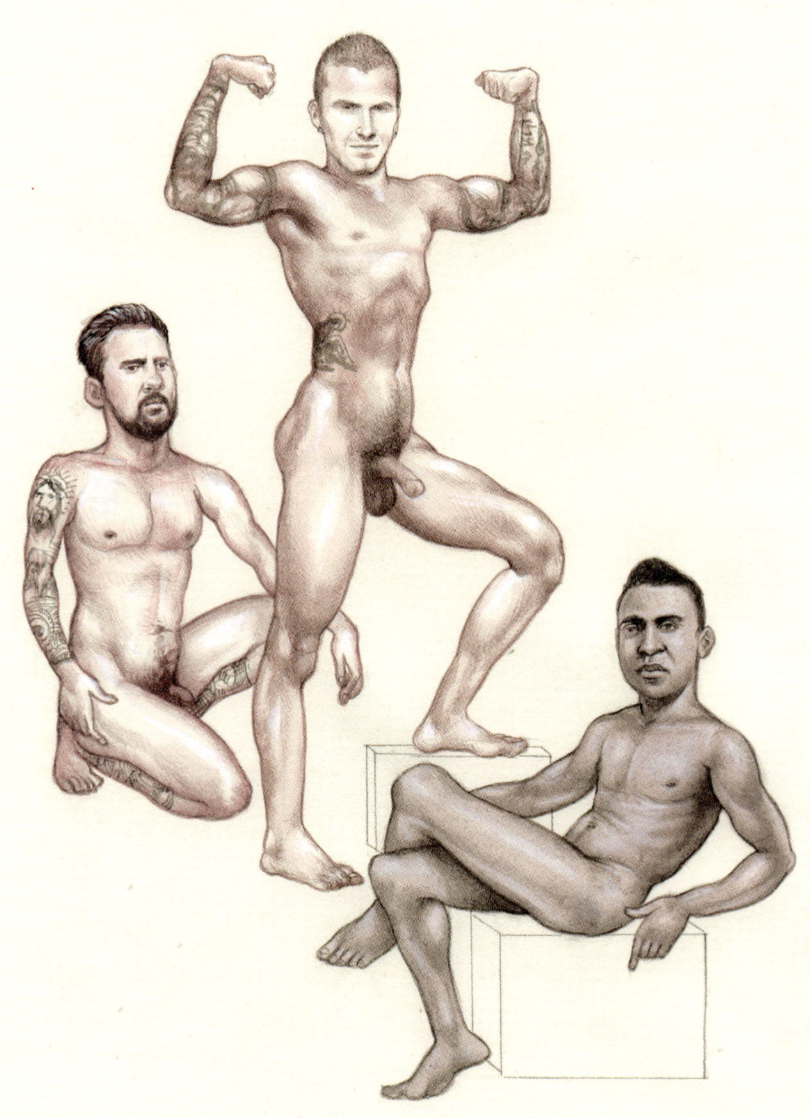

THE FOOTBALLERS

Lionel Messi, David Beckham & Pelé

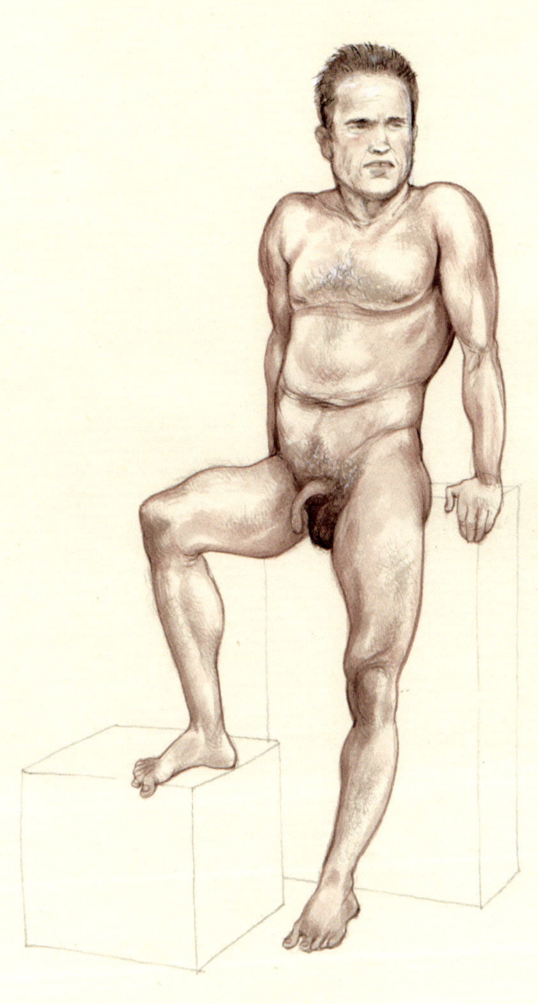

Arnold Schwarzenegger

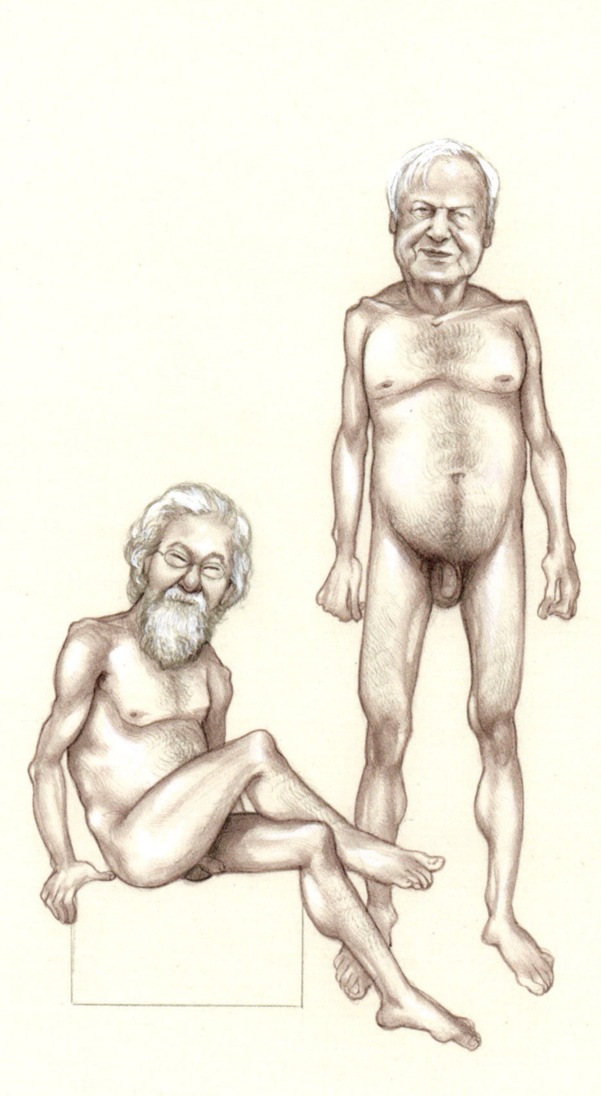

THE SAVIOURS

David Suzuki & David Attenborough

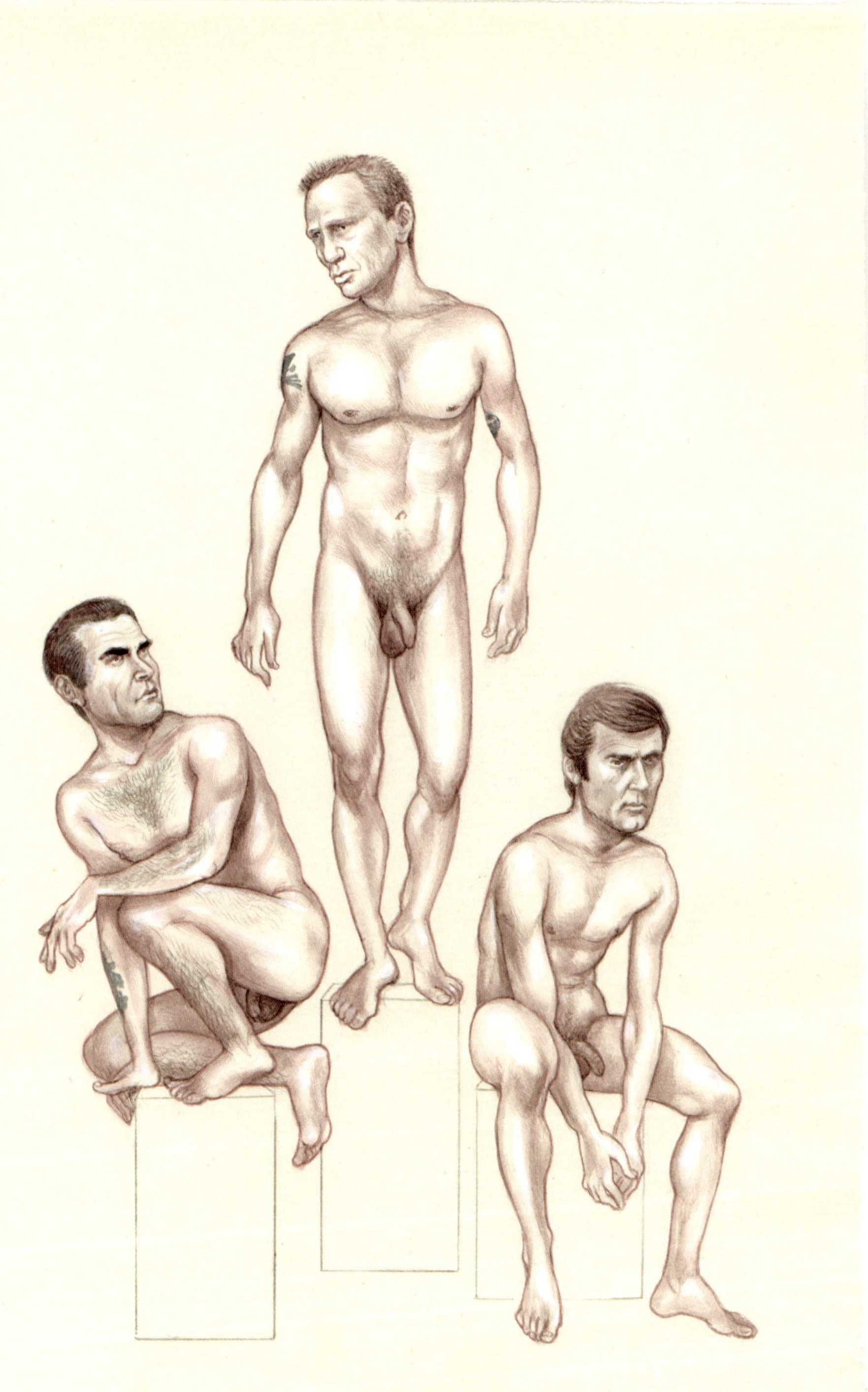

THE BOND MEN

Sean Connery, Daniel Craig & Roger Moore

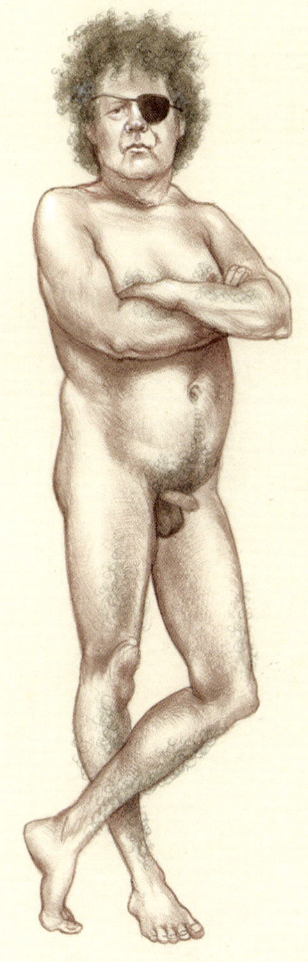

Dale Chihuly

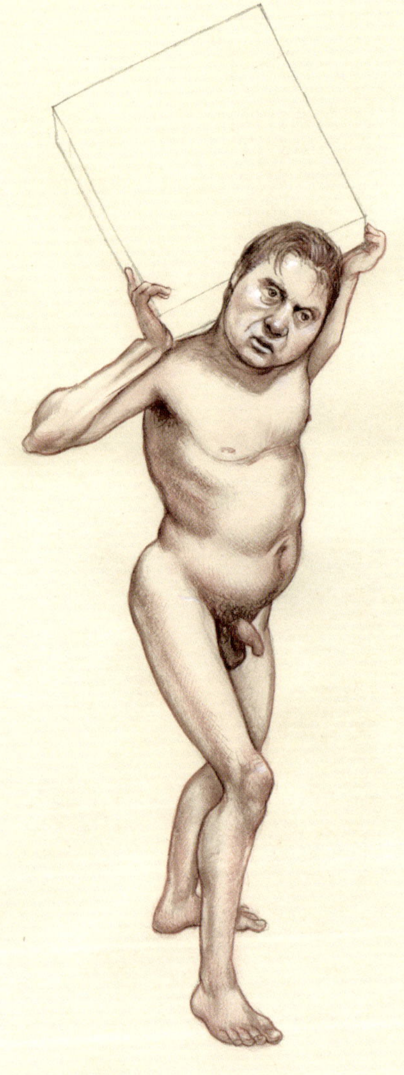

Francis Bacon

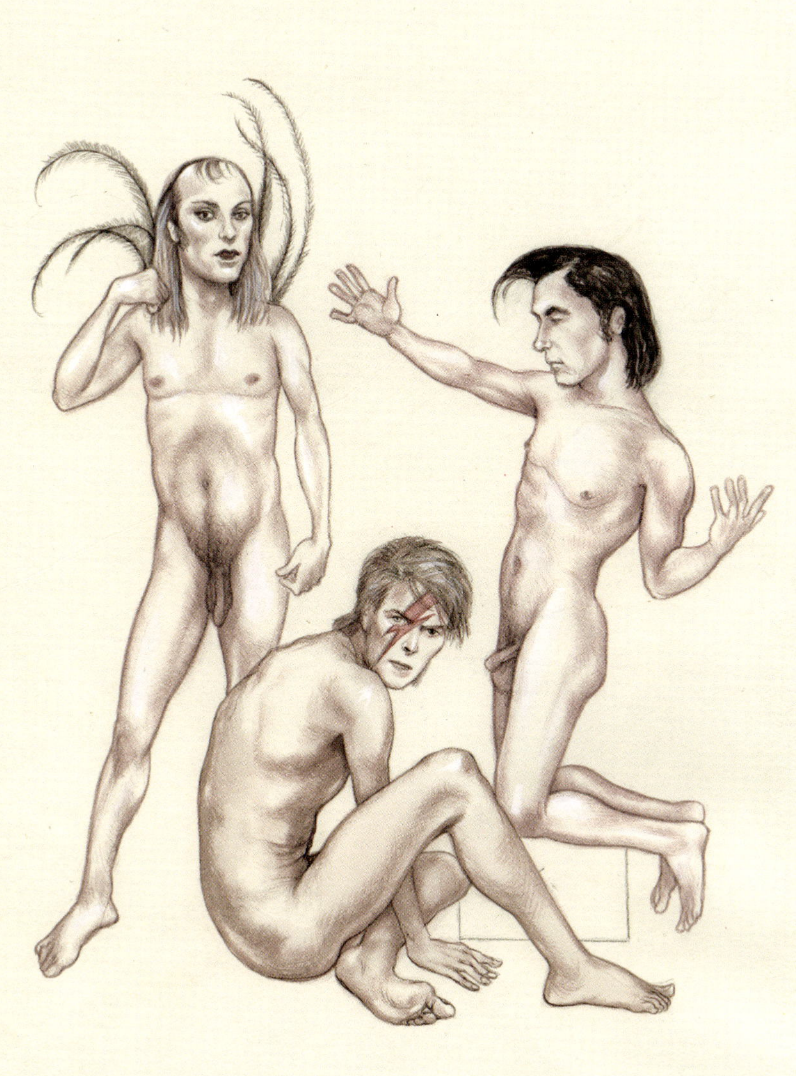

THE GLAM ROCKERS

Brian Eno, David Bowie & Bryan Ferry

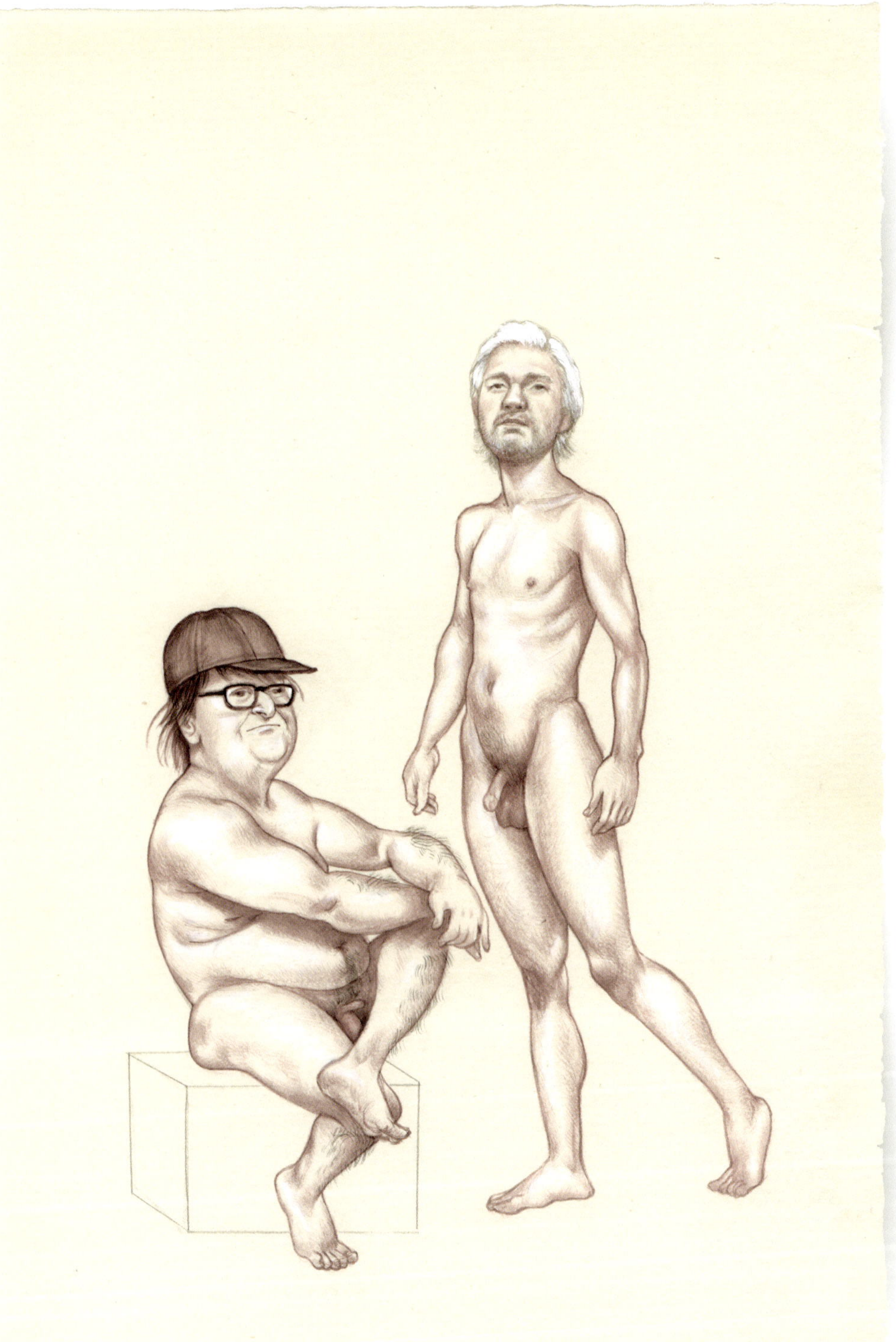

THE AGITATORS

Michael Moore & Julian Assange

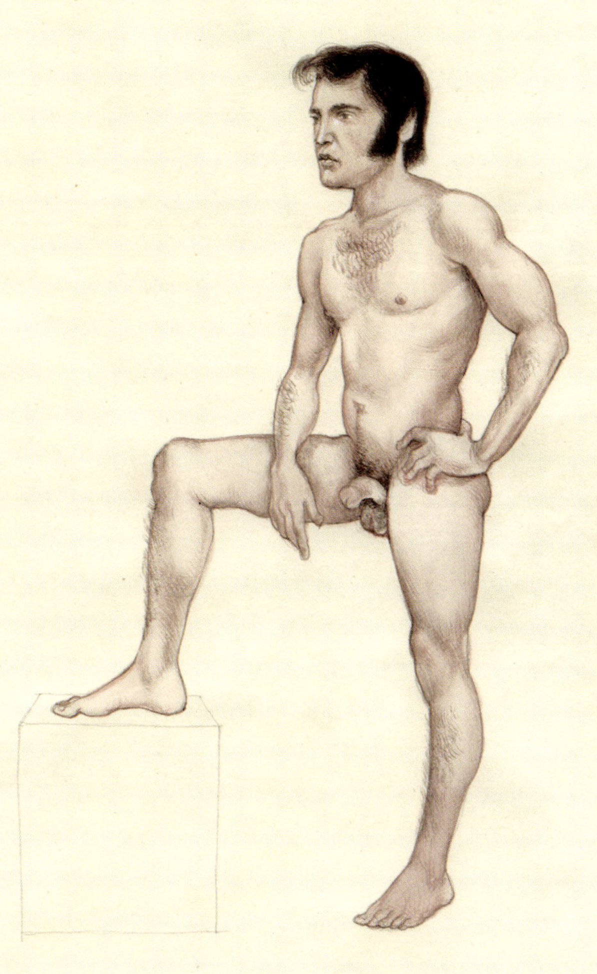

Elvis Presley

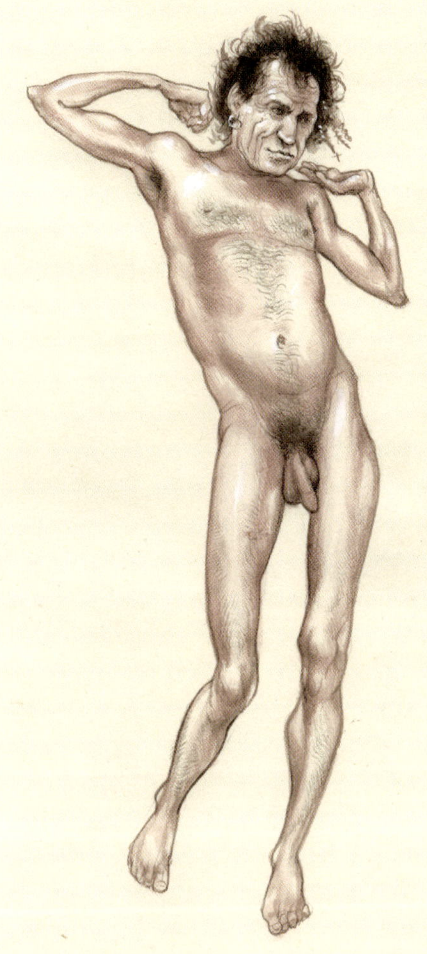

Keith Richards

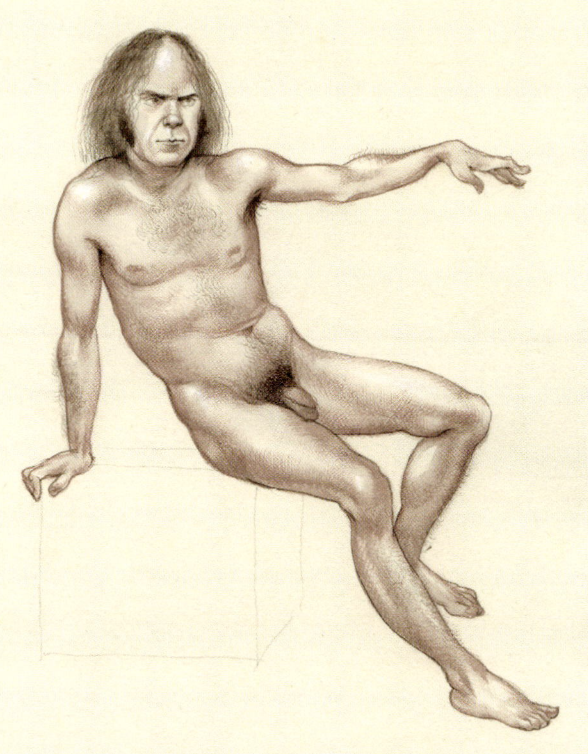

Neil Young

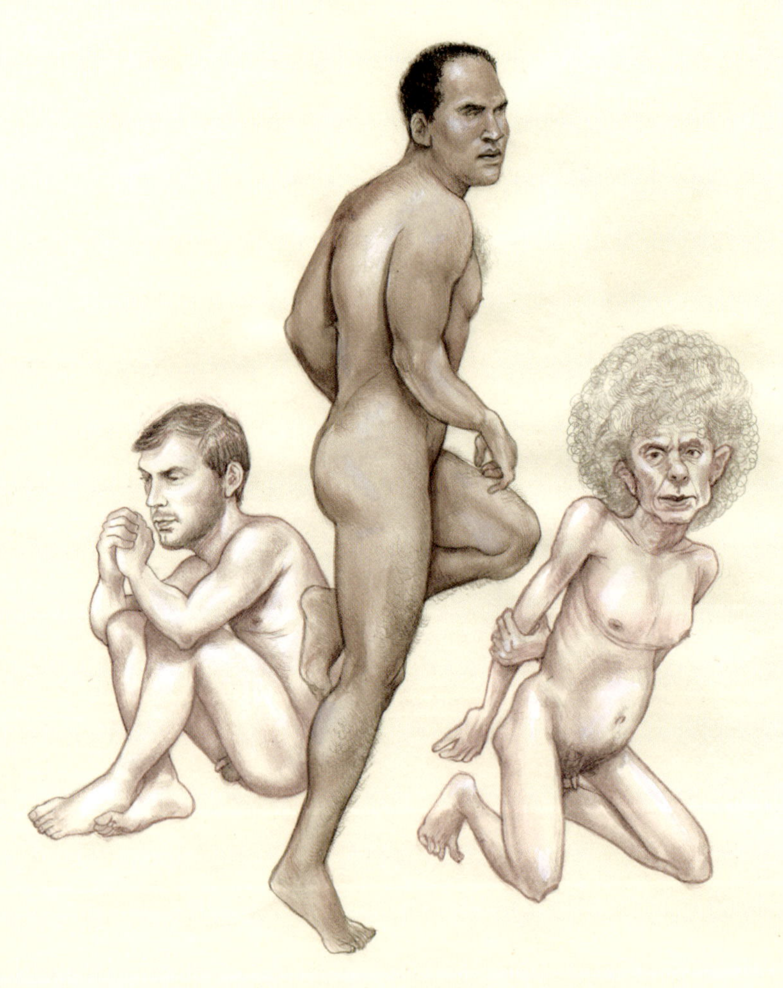

THE KILLERS

Jeffrey Dahmer, OJ Simpson & Phil Spector

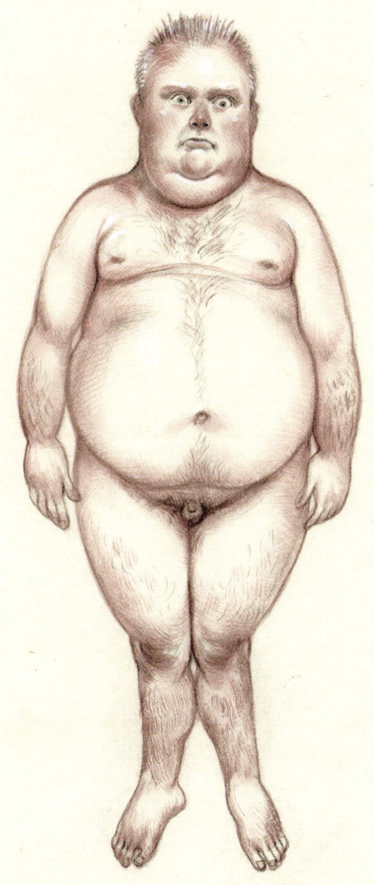

Rob Ford

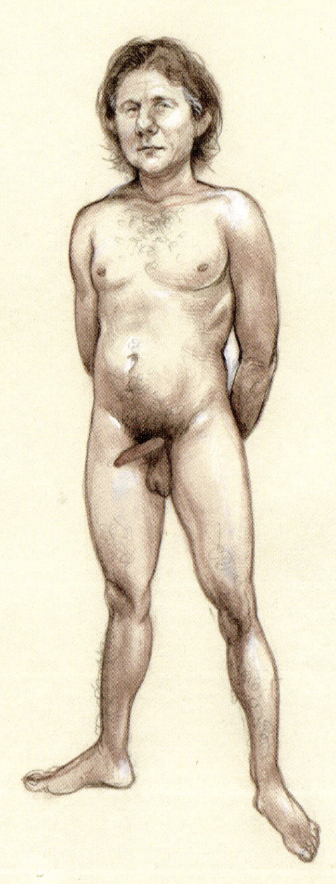

Roman Polanski

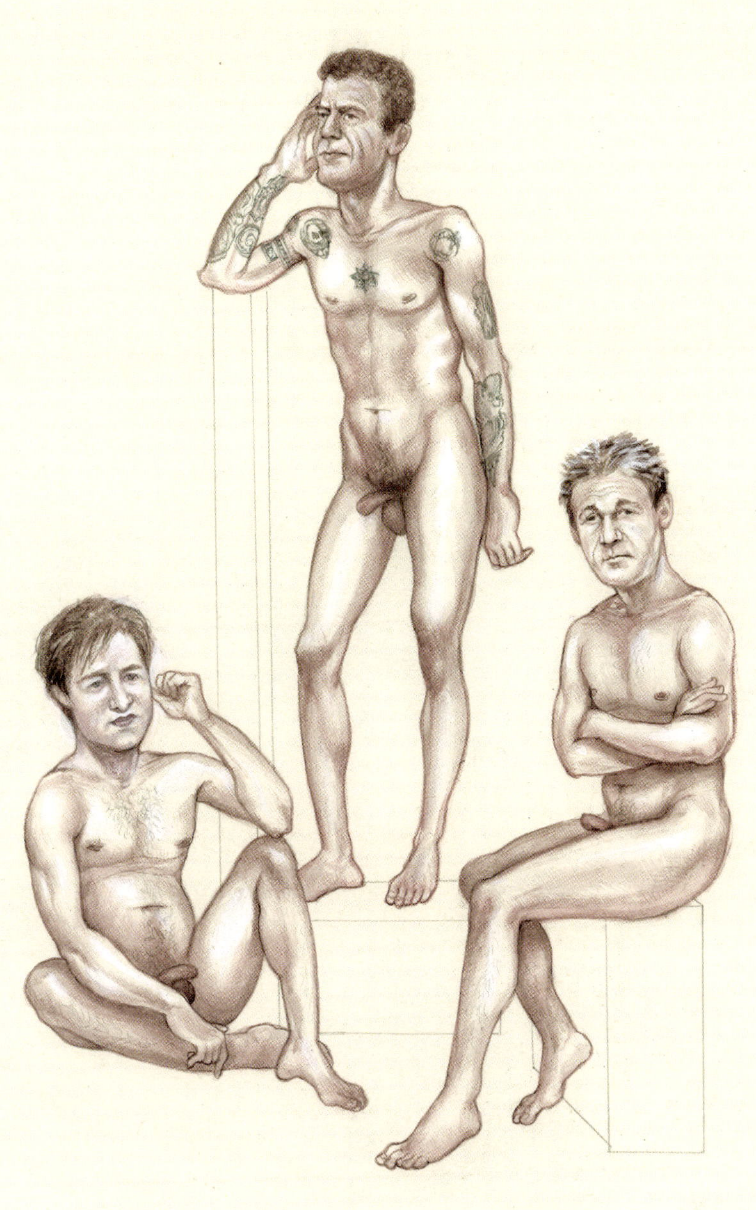

THE CHEFS

Jamie Oliver, Anthony Bourdain & Gordon Ramsay

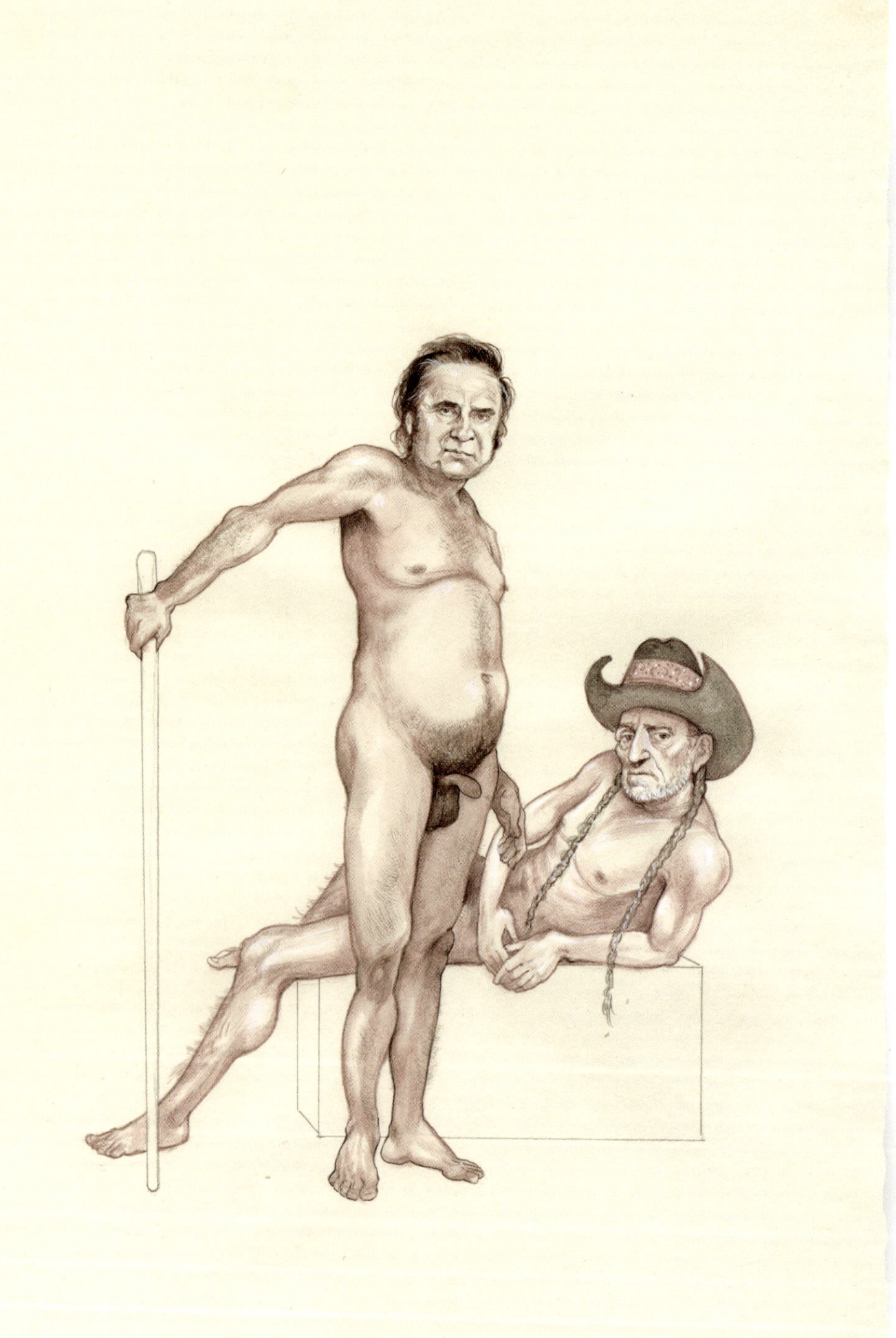

THE COUNTRY SINGERS

Johnny Cash & Willie Nelson

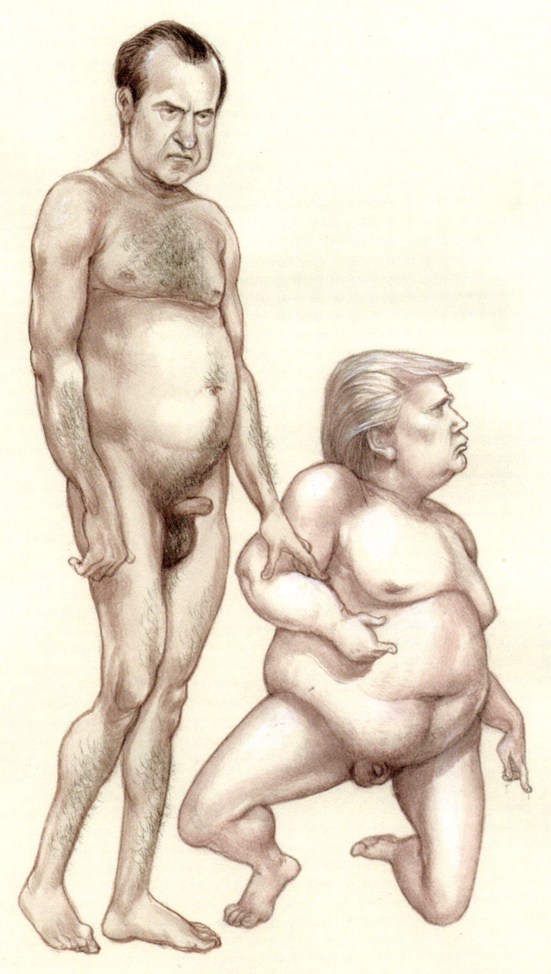

THE CROOKS

Richard Nixon & Donald Trump

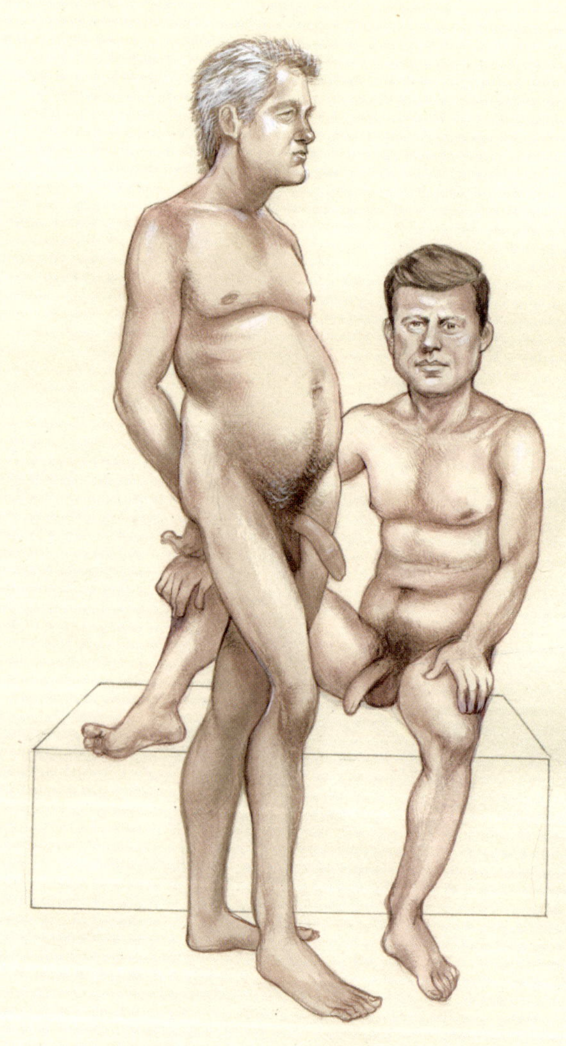

THE DEMOCRATS

Bill Clinton & John F. Kennedy

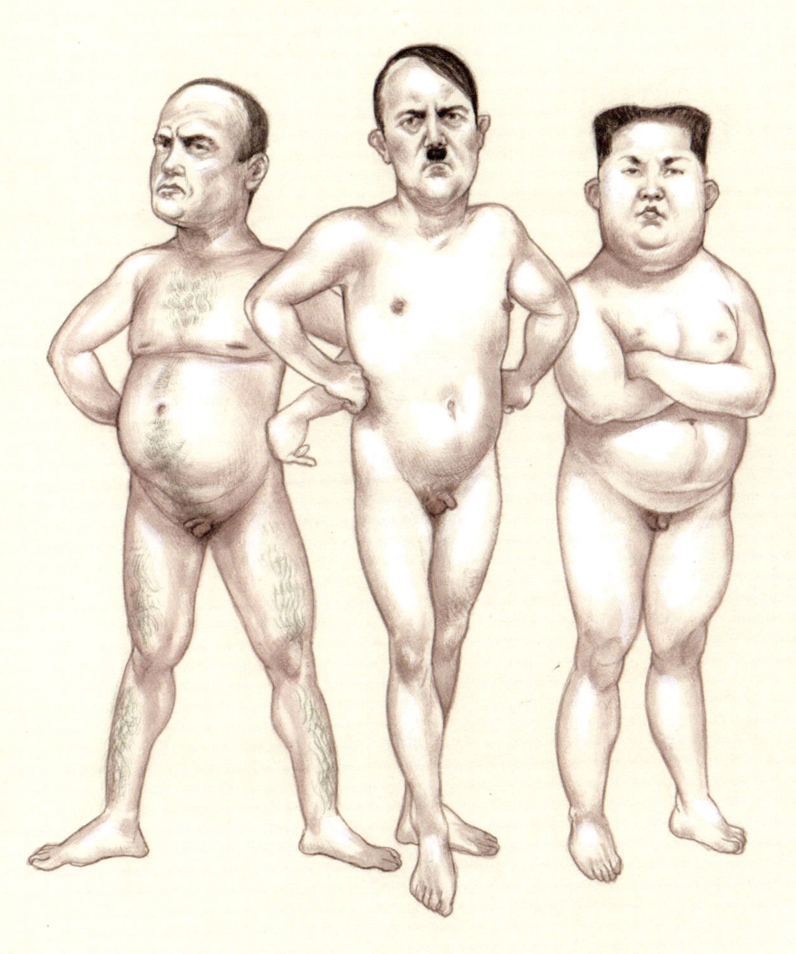

THE DICTATORS

Silvio Berlusconi, Adolf Hitler & Kim Jong Un

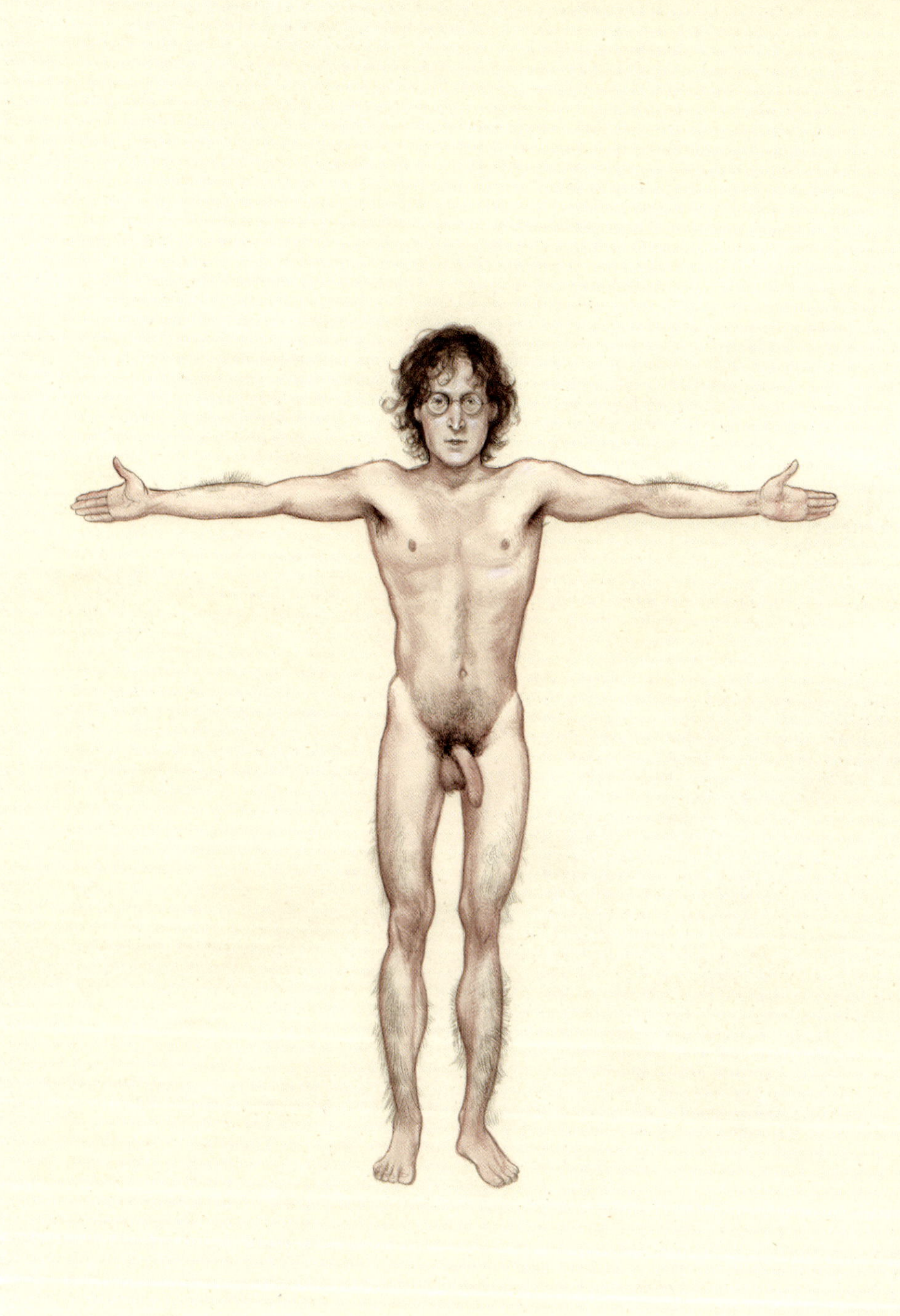

John Lennon

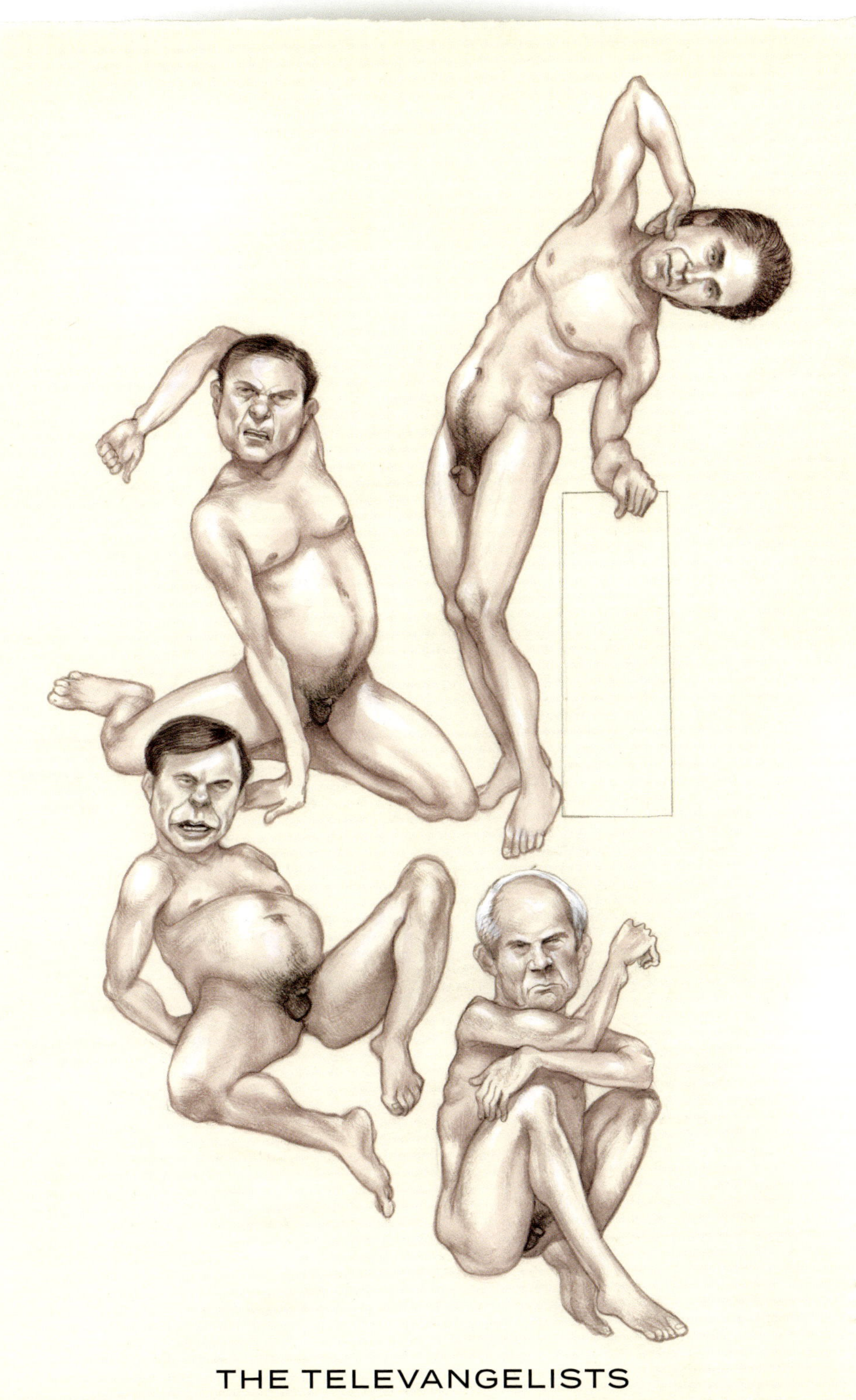

THE TELEVANGELISTS

Kenneth Copeland, Joel Osteen, Jim Bakker & Pat Robertson

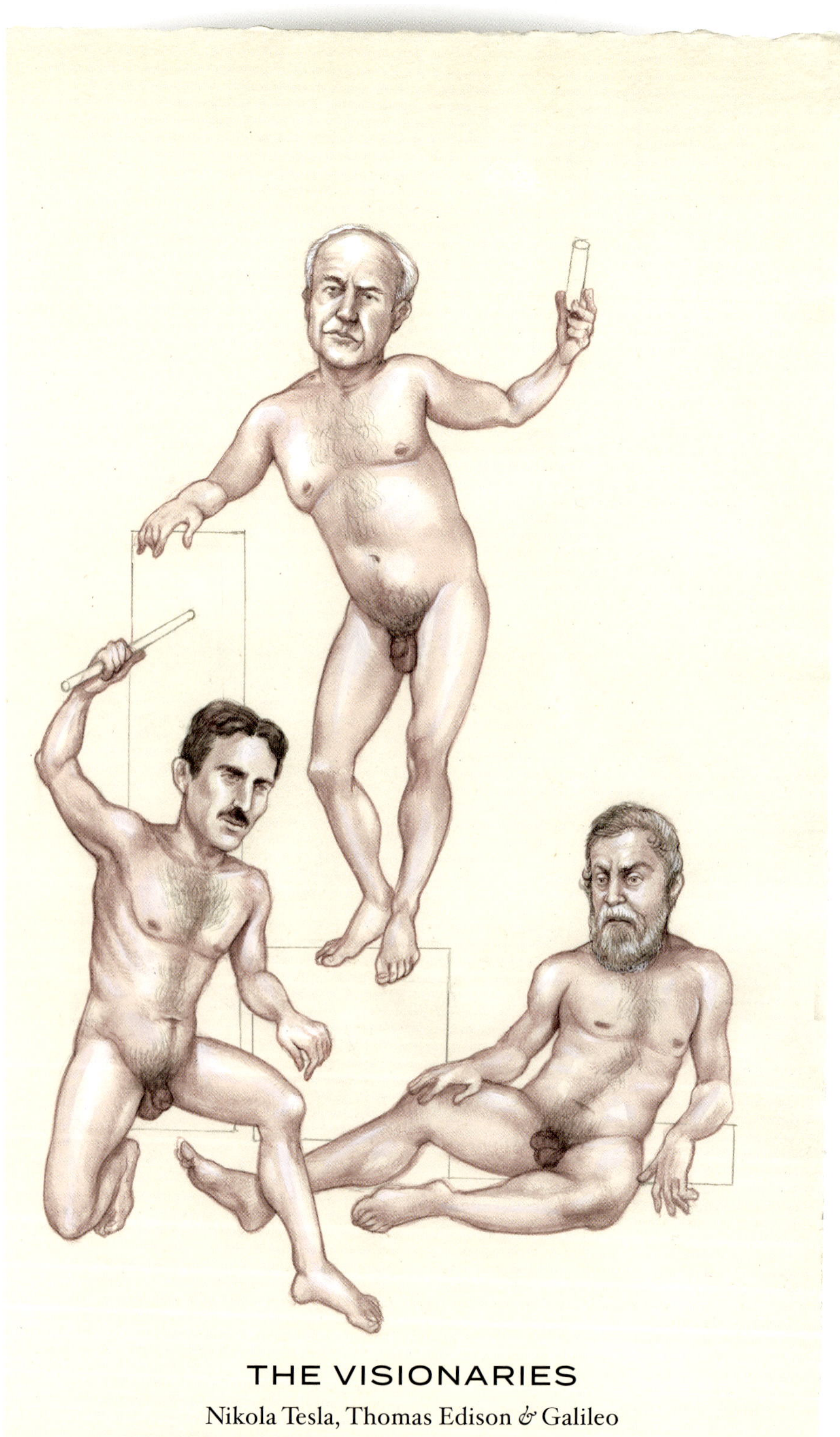

THE VISIONARIES
Nikola Tesla, Thomas Edison & Galileo

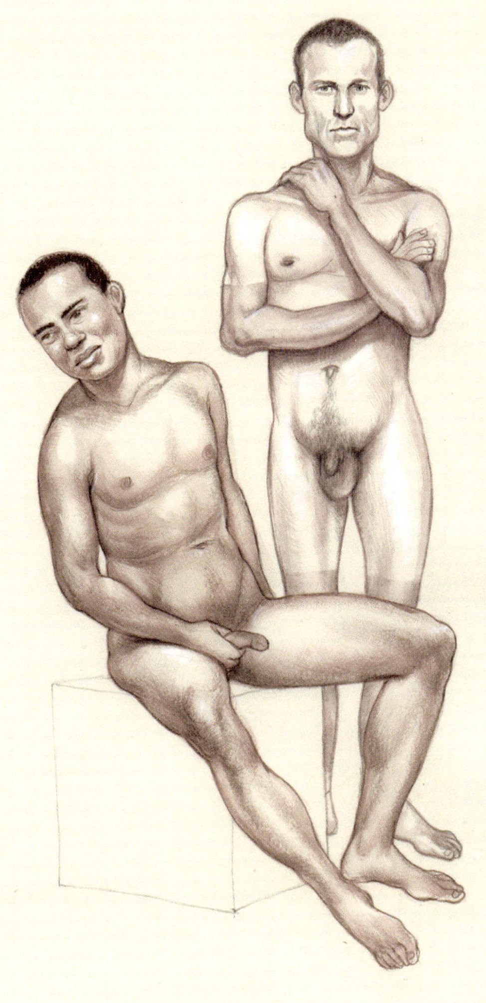

THE DISGRACED

Tiger Wood & Lance Armstrong

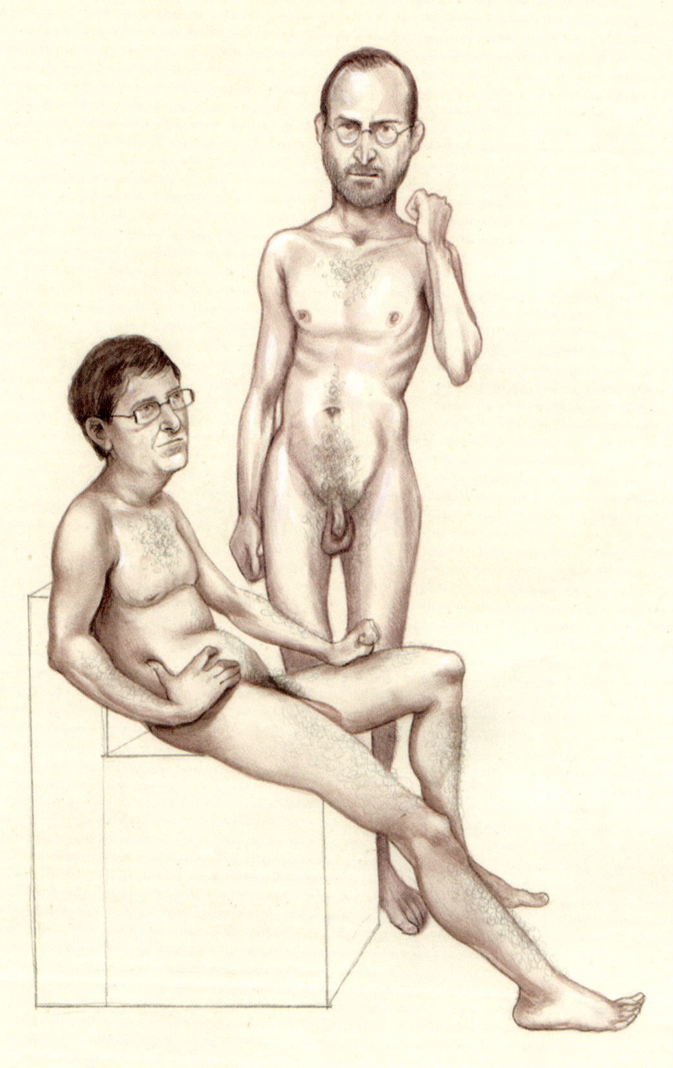

THE INNOVATORS

Bill Gates & Steve Jobs

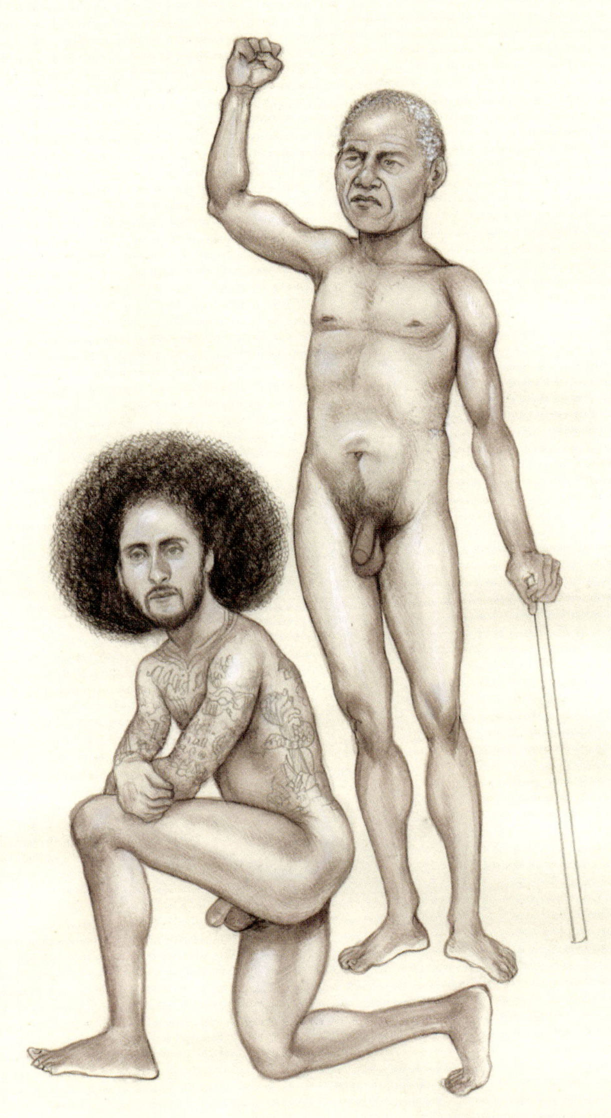

THE SOCIAL JUSTICE WARRIORS

Colin Kaepernick & Nelson Mandela

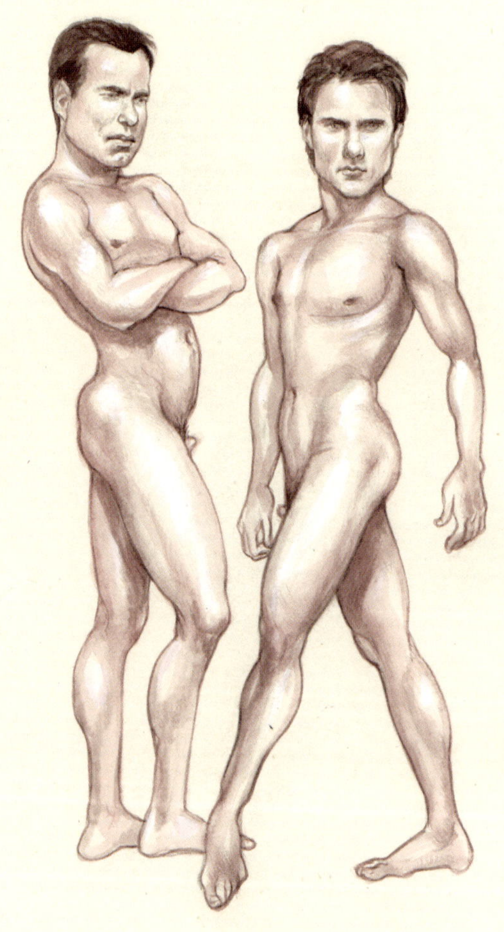

THE SCIENTOLOGISTS

John Travolta *&* Tom Cruise

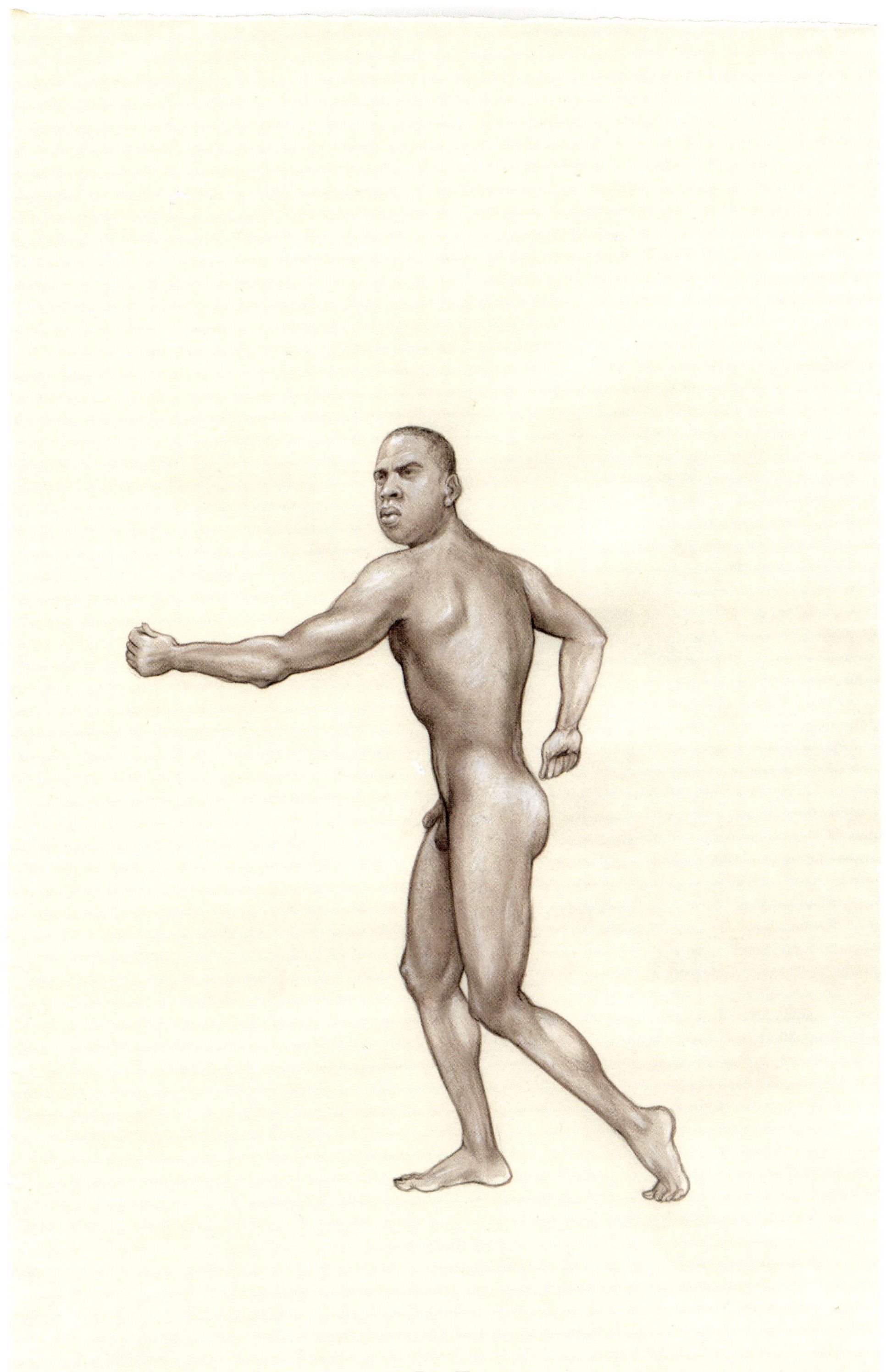

Jay-Z

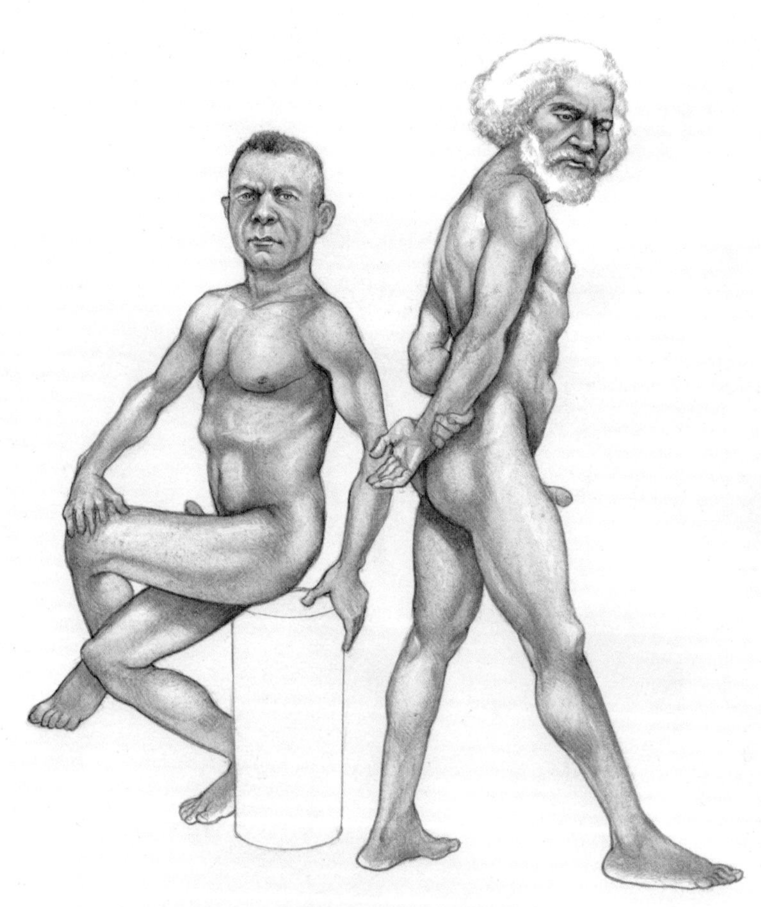

THE LEADERS

Booker T. Washington & Frederick Douglass

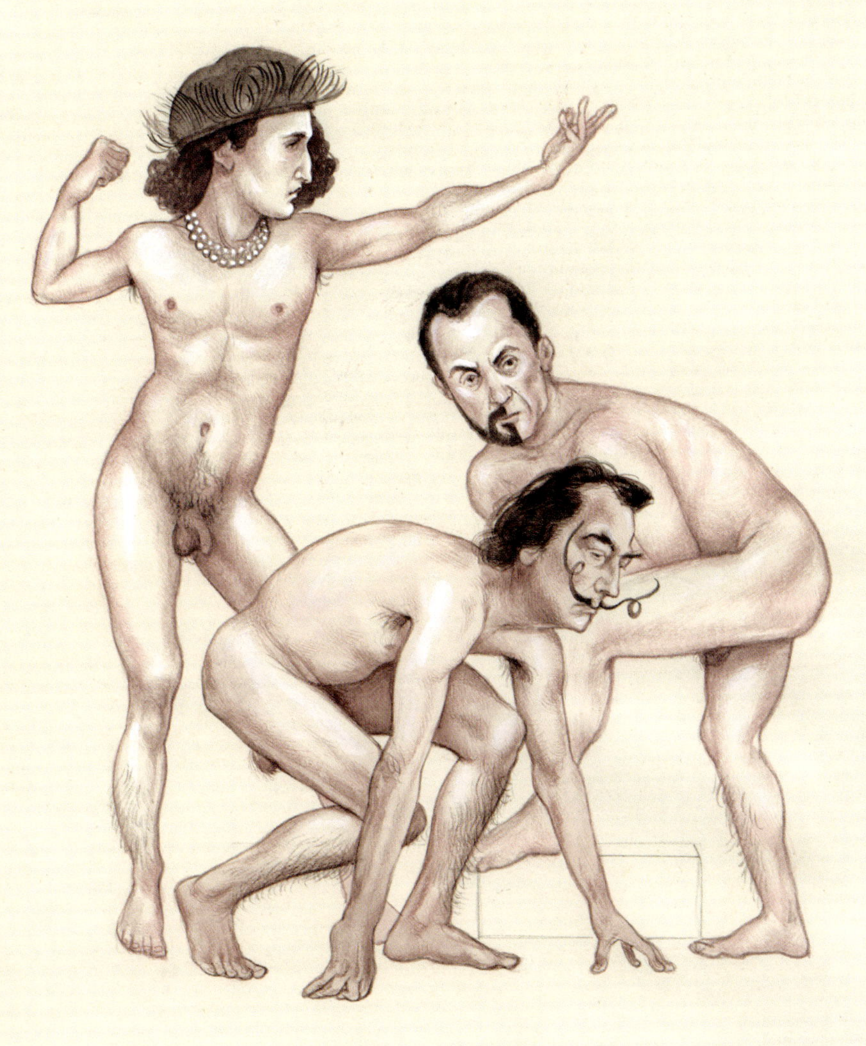

THE SURREALISTS

Marcel Duchamp, Salvador Dali & Man Ray

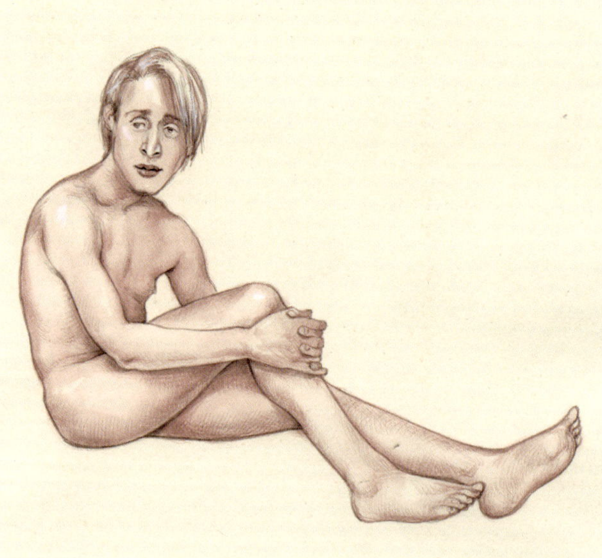

Macaulay Culkin

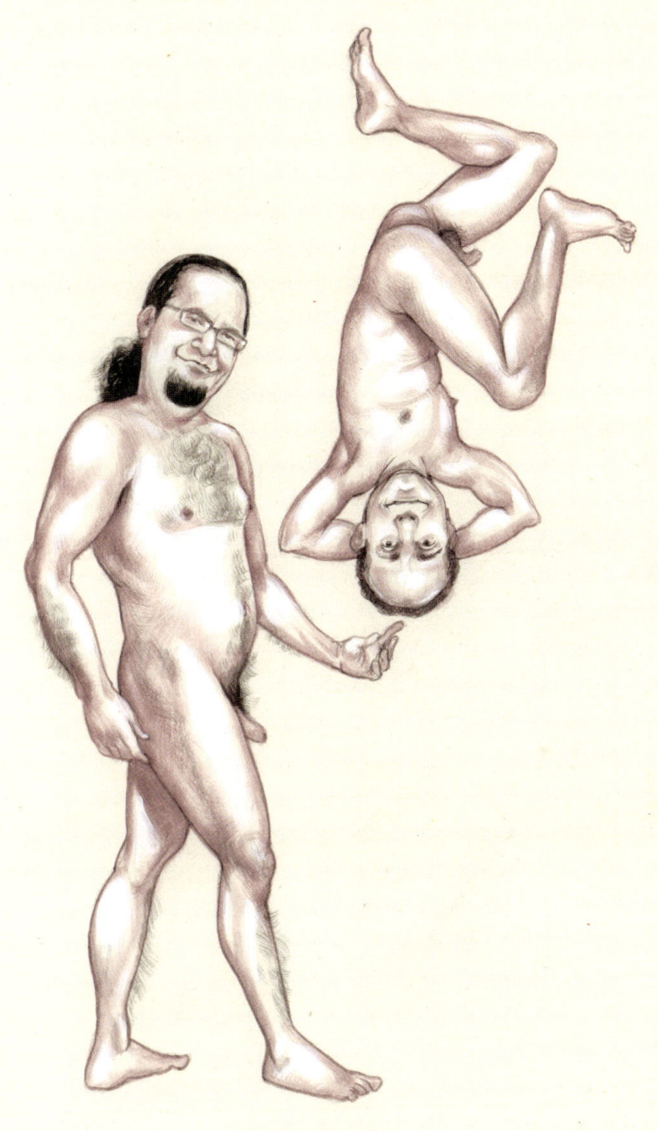

THE MAGICIANS

Penn & Teller

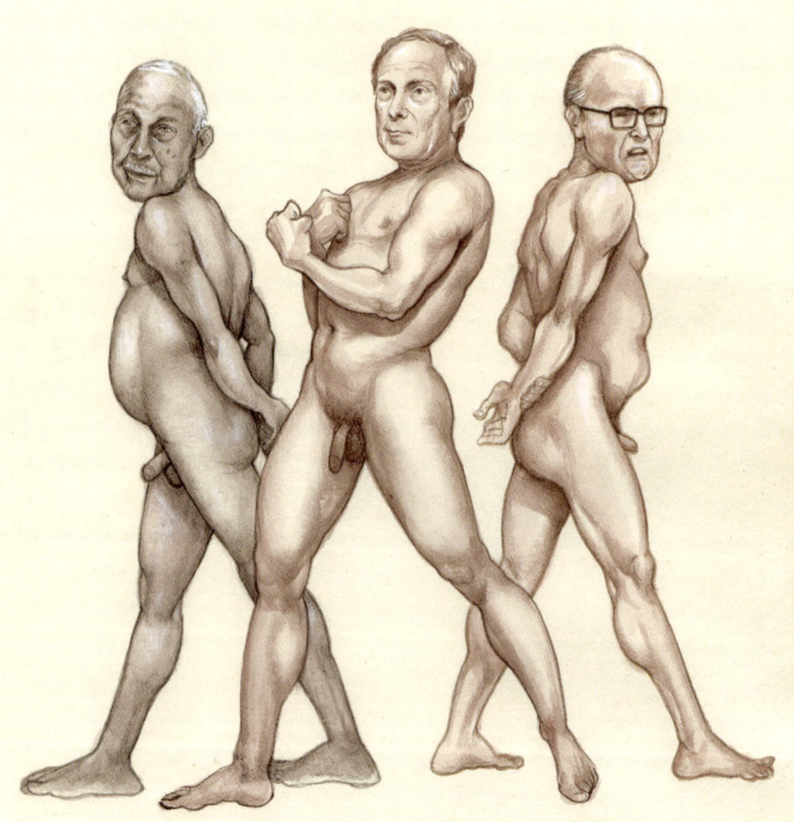

THE NY MAYORS

David Dinkins, Michael Bloomberg & Rudy Giuliani

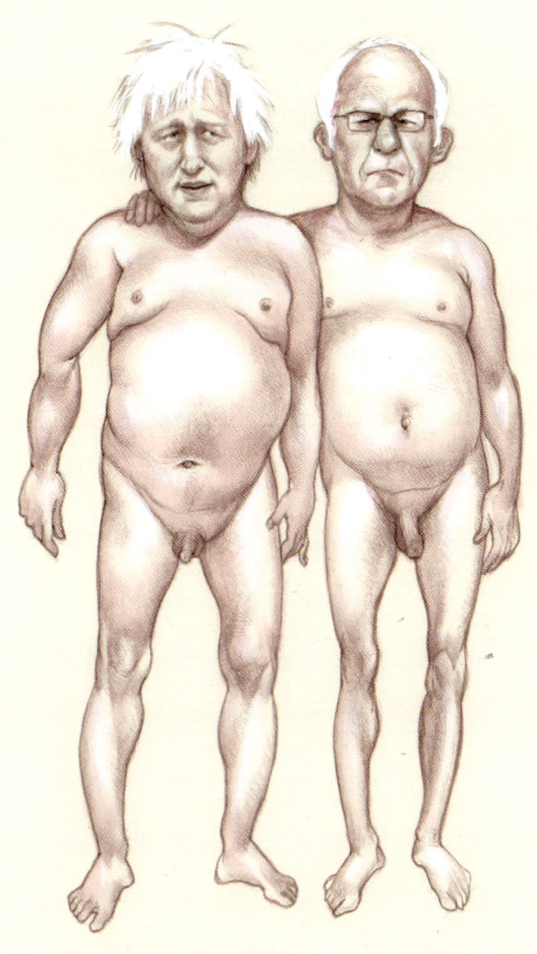

THE OPPOSITES

Boris Johnson & Bernie Sanders

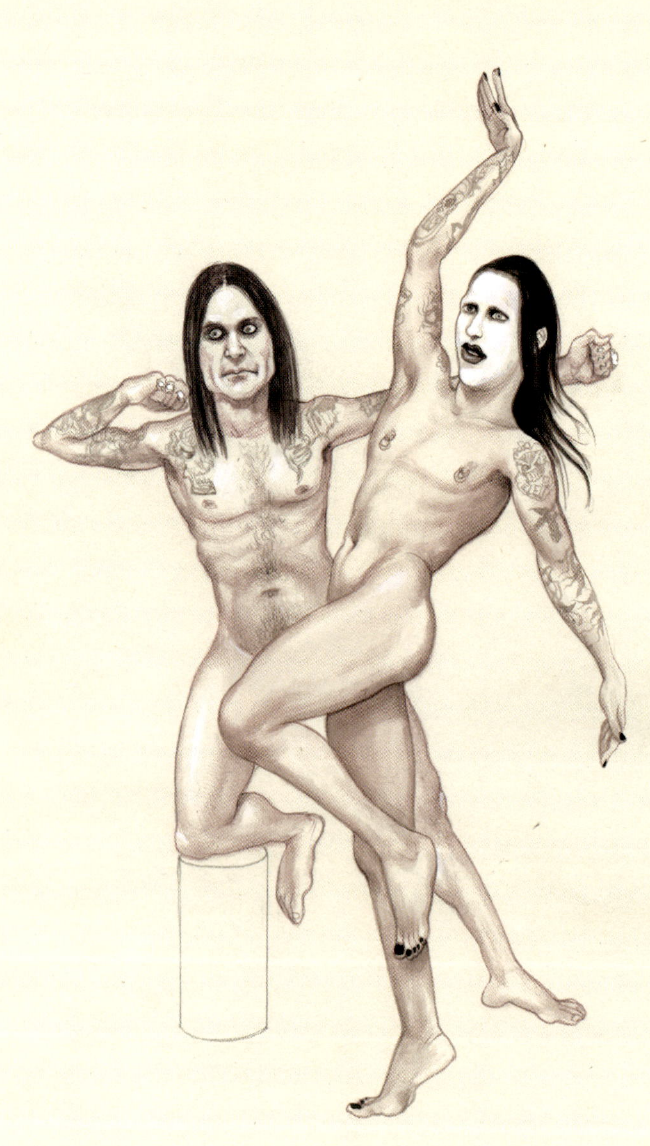

THE METALHEADS

Ozzy Osbourne *&* Marilyn Manson

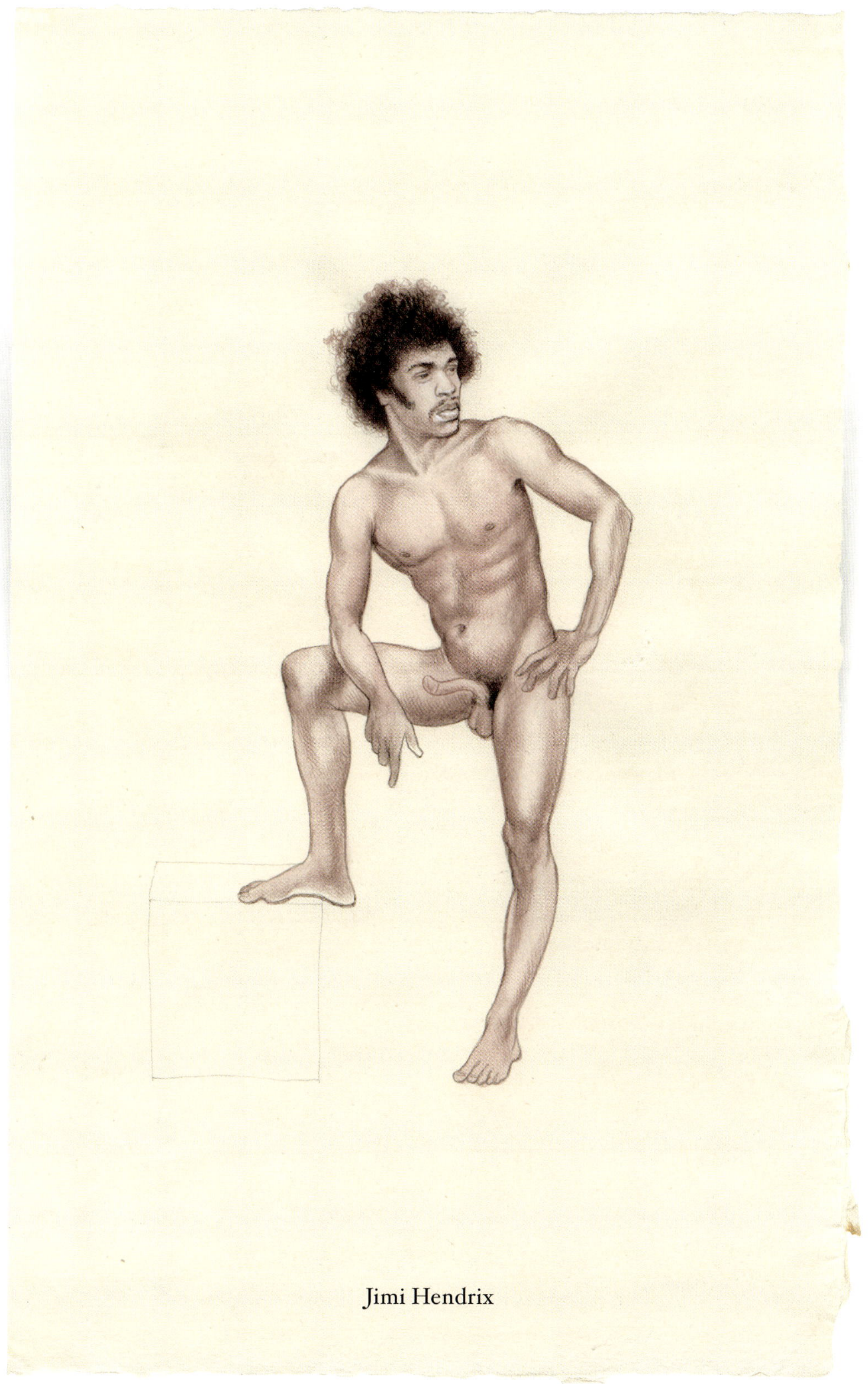

Jimi Hendrix

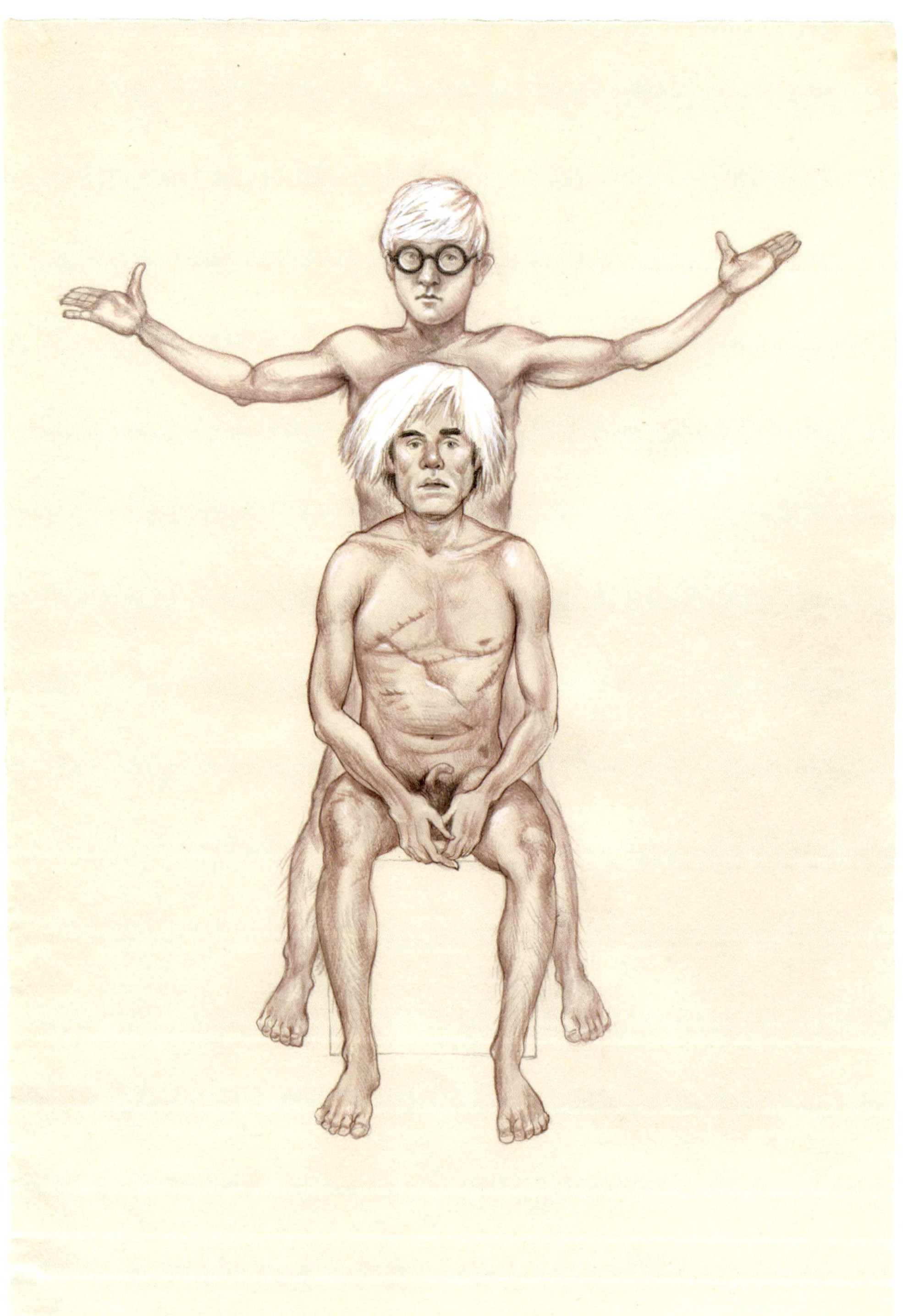

THE MODERN ARTISTS

David Hockney *&* Andy Warhol

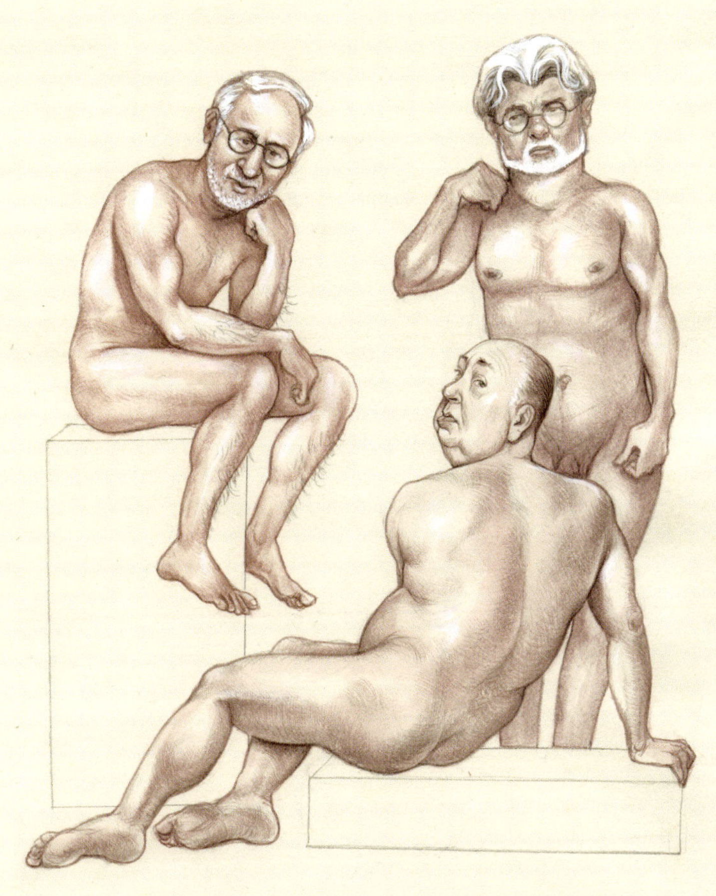

THE MOVIE MAKERS

Steven Spielberg, Alfred Hitchcock *&* George Lucas

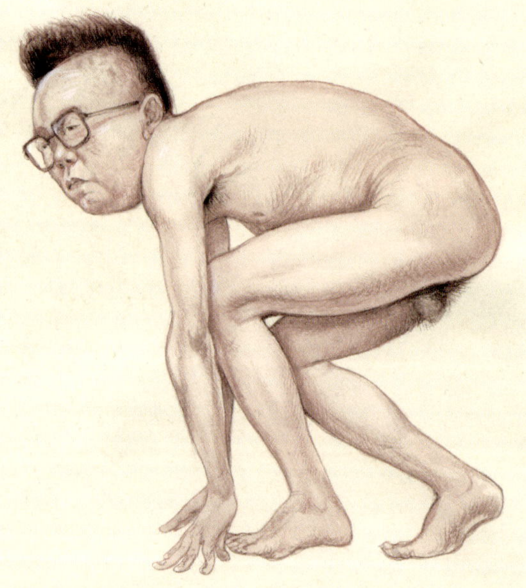

Kim Jong Il

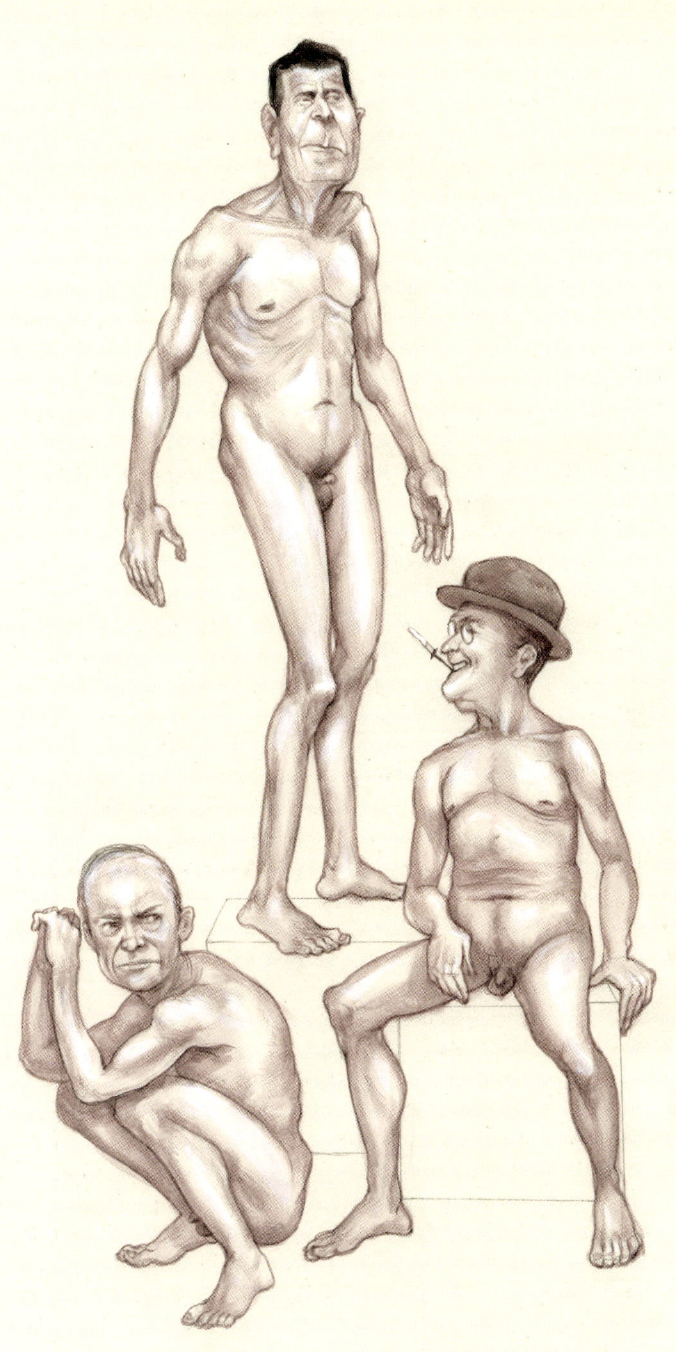

THE PRESIDENTS

Dwight D. Eisenhower, Ronald Reagan & Franklin D. Roosevelt

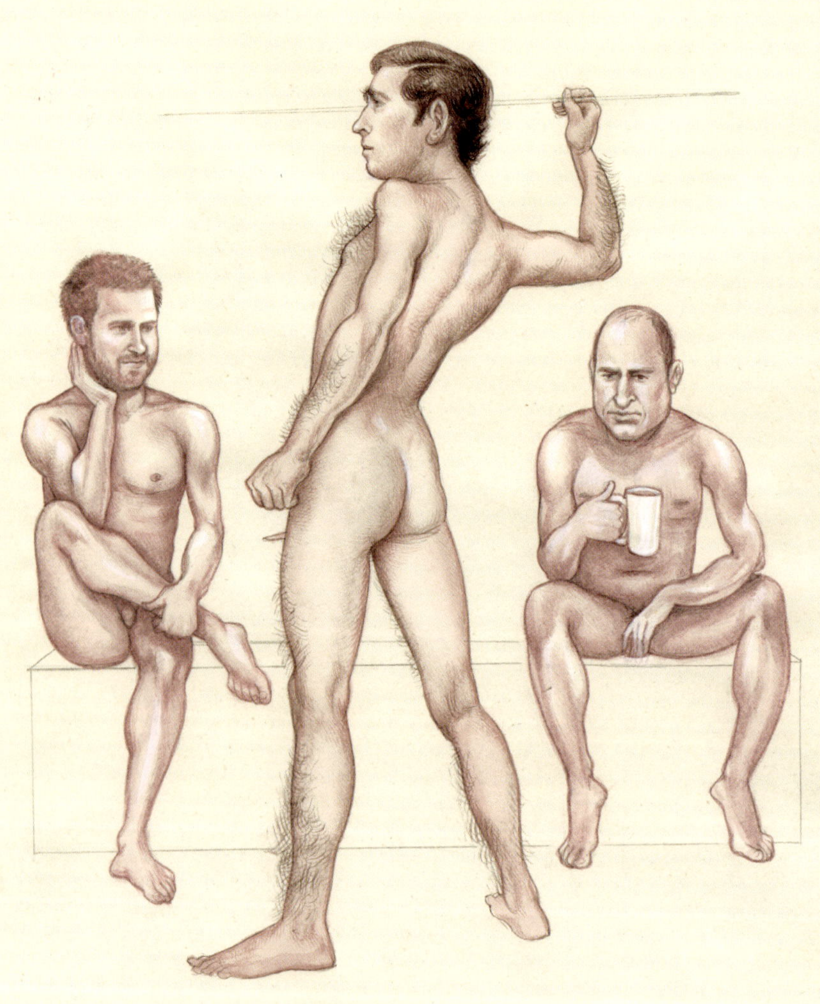

THE KING, THE HEIR AND THE SPARE

Prince Harry, King Charles *&* Prince William

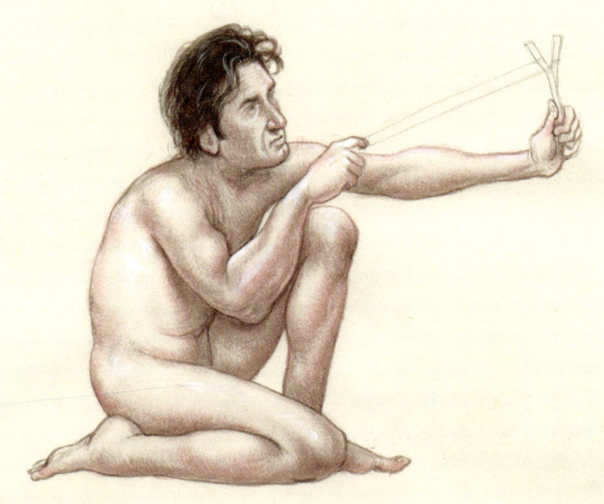

Sean Penn

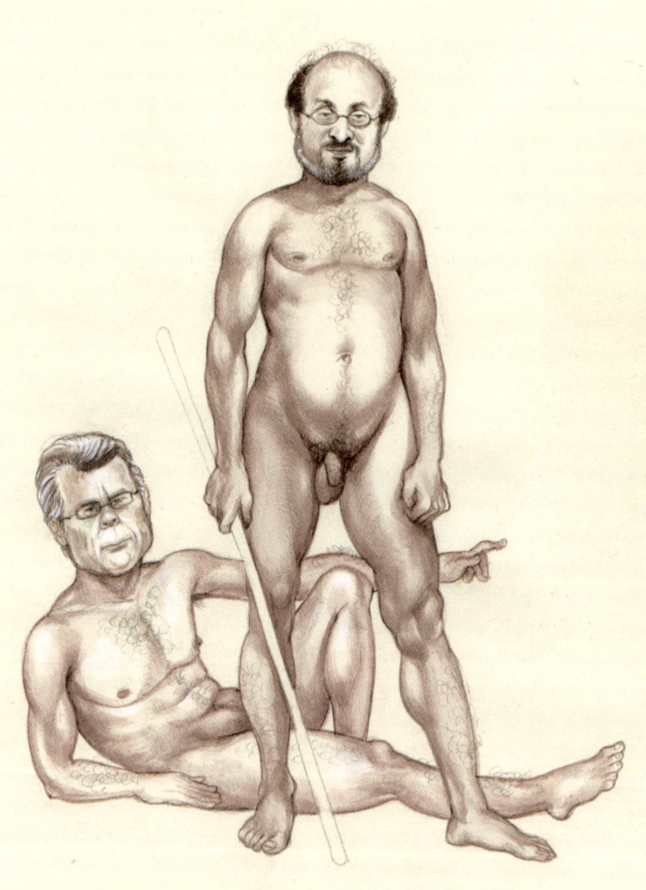

THE WRITERS

Stephen King & Salman Rushdie

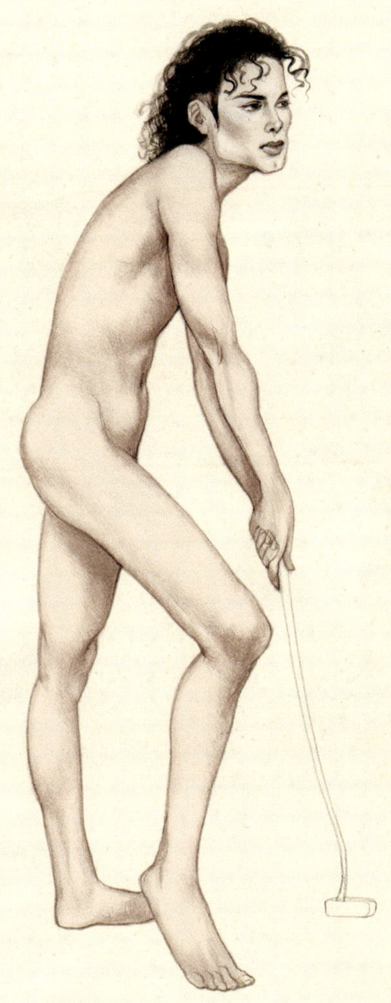

Michael Jackson

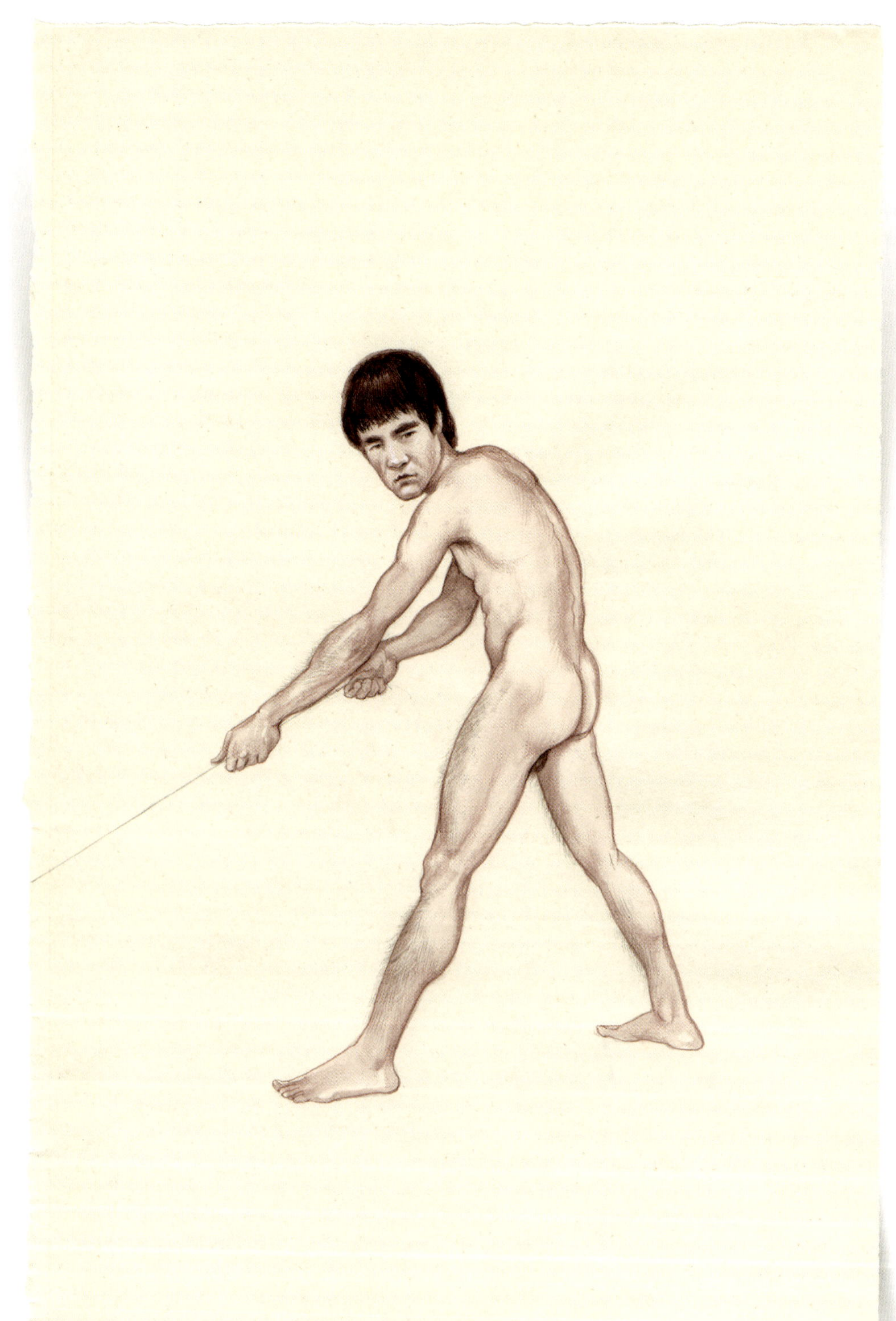

Bruce Lee

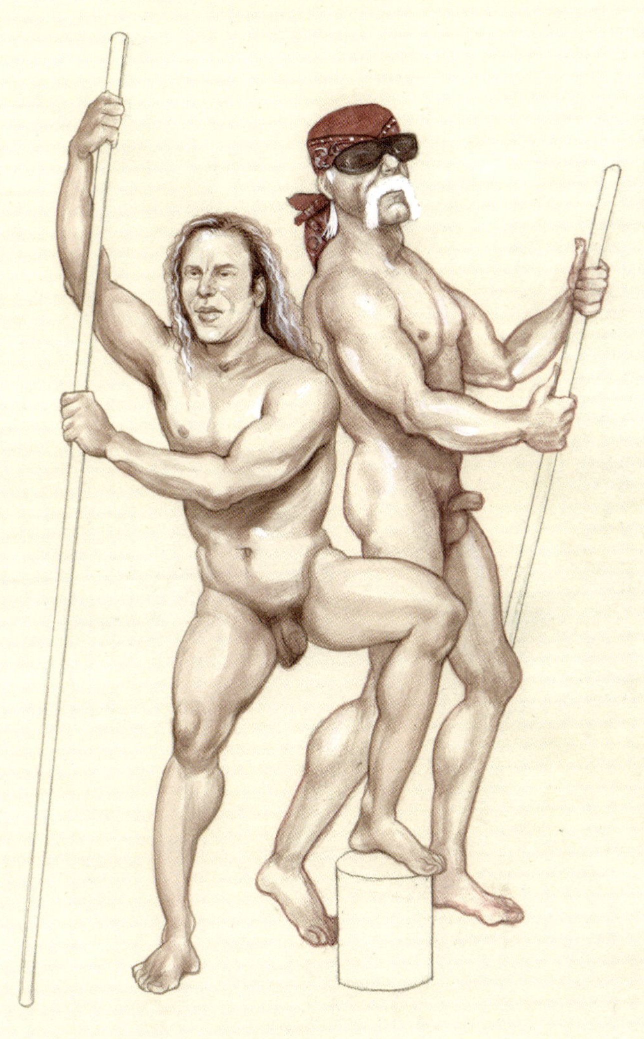

THE WRESTLERS

Mickey Rourke & Hulk Hogan

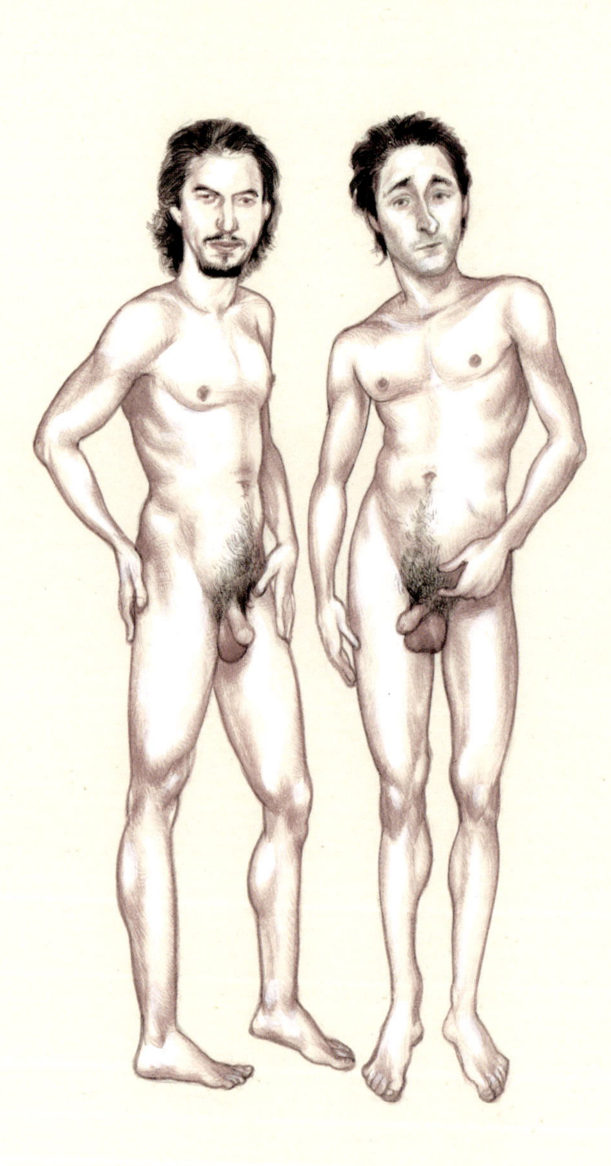

THE YOUNG GUNS

Adam Driver & Adrien Brody

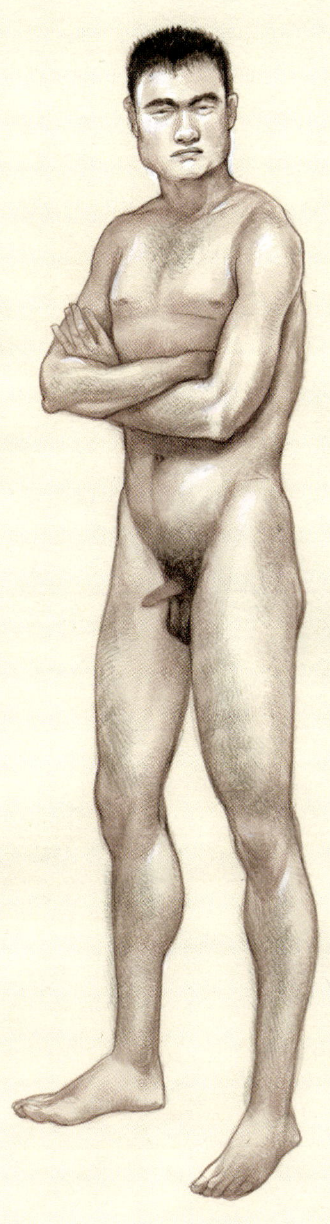

Yao Ming

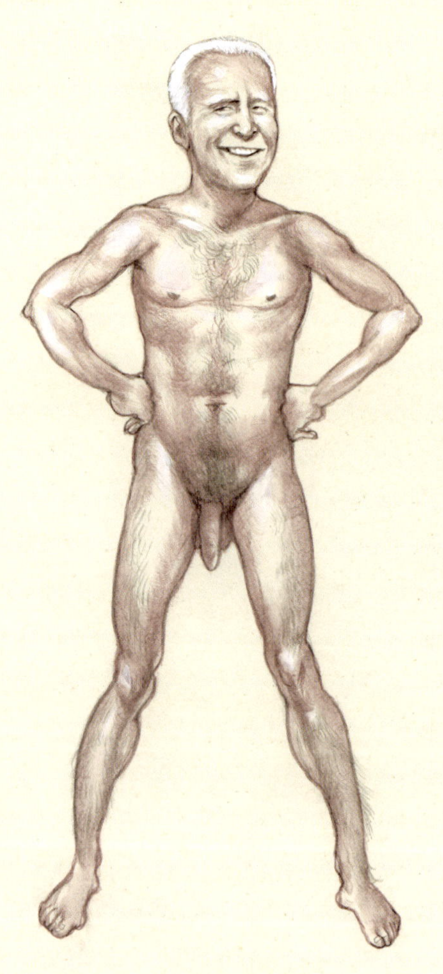

THE WINNER
Joe Biden

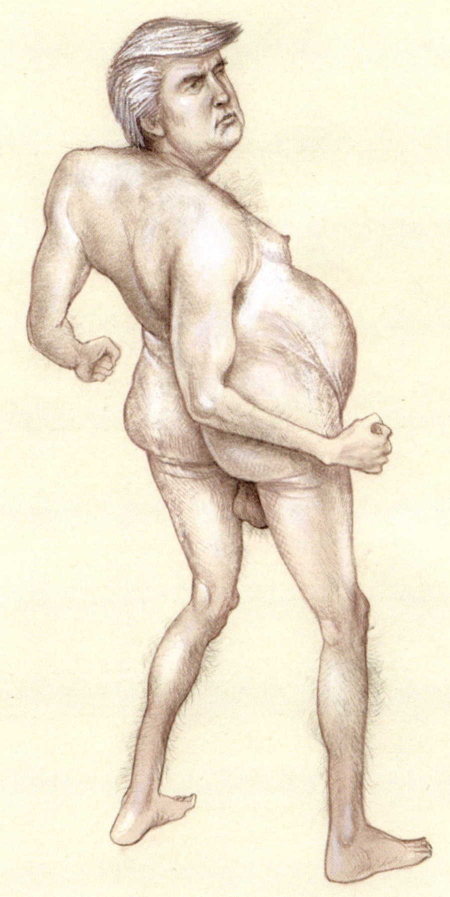

THE LOSER

Donald Trump

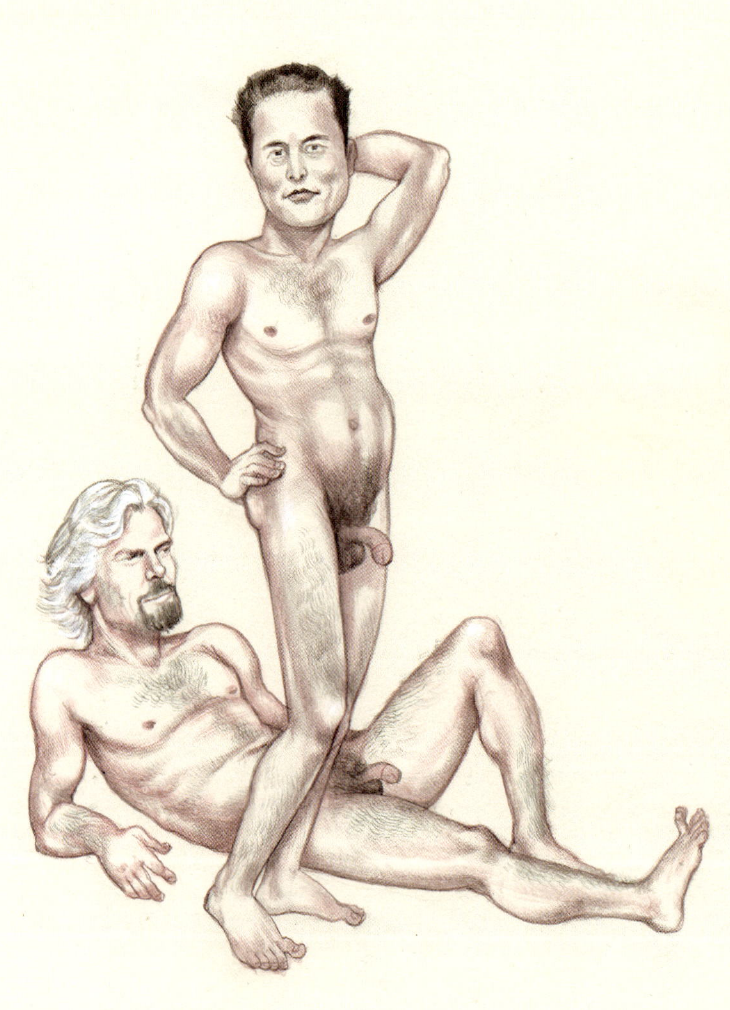

THE UBER WEALTHY

Richard Branson & Elon Musk

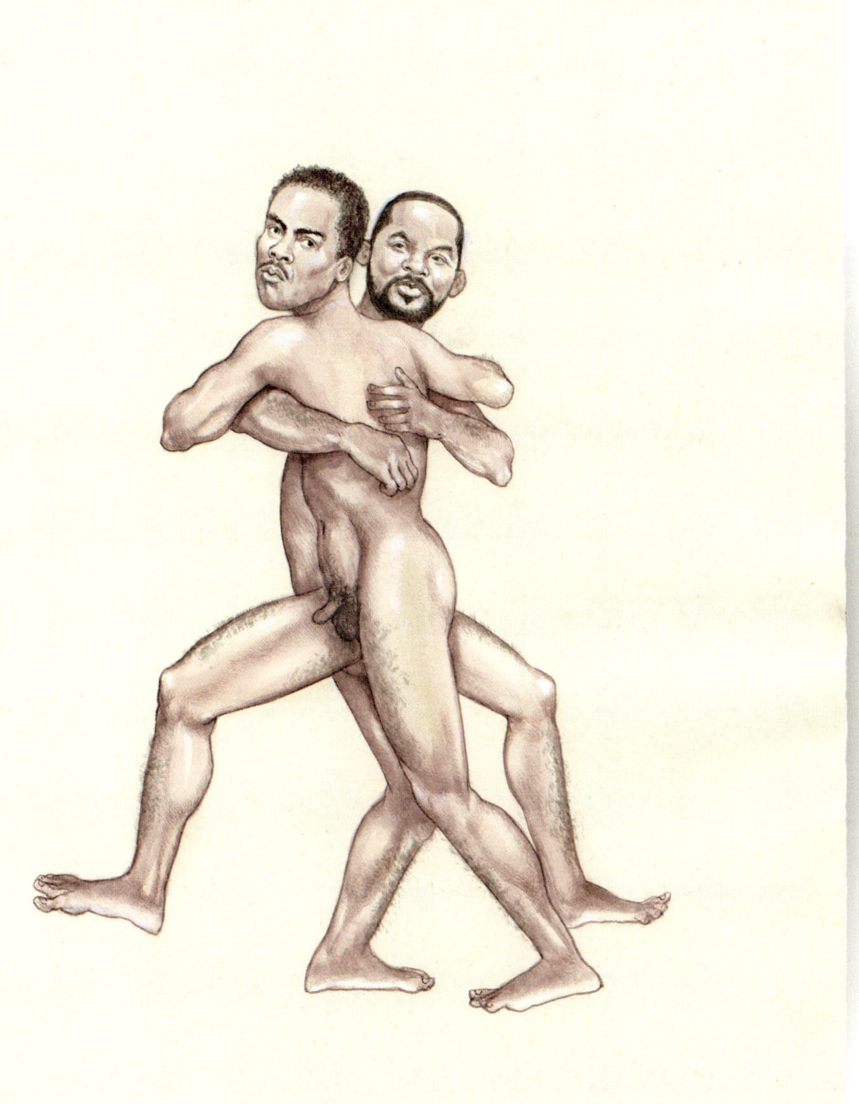

Chris Rock *&* Will Smith

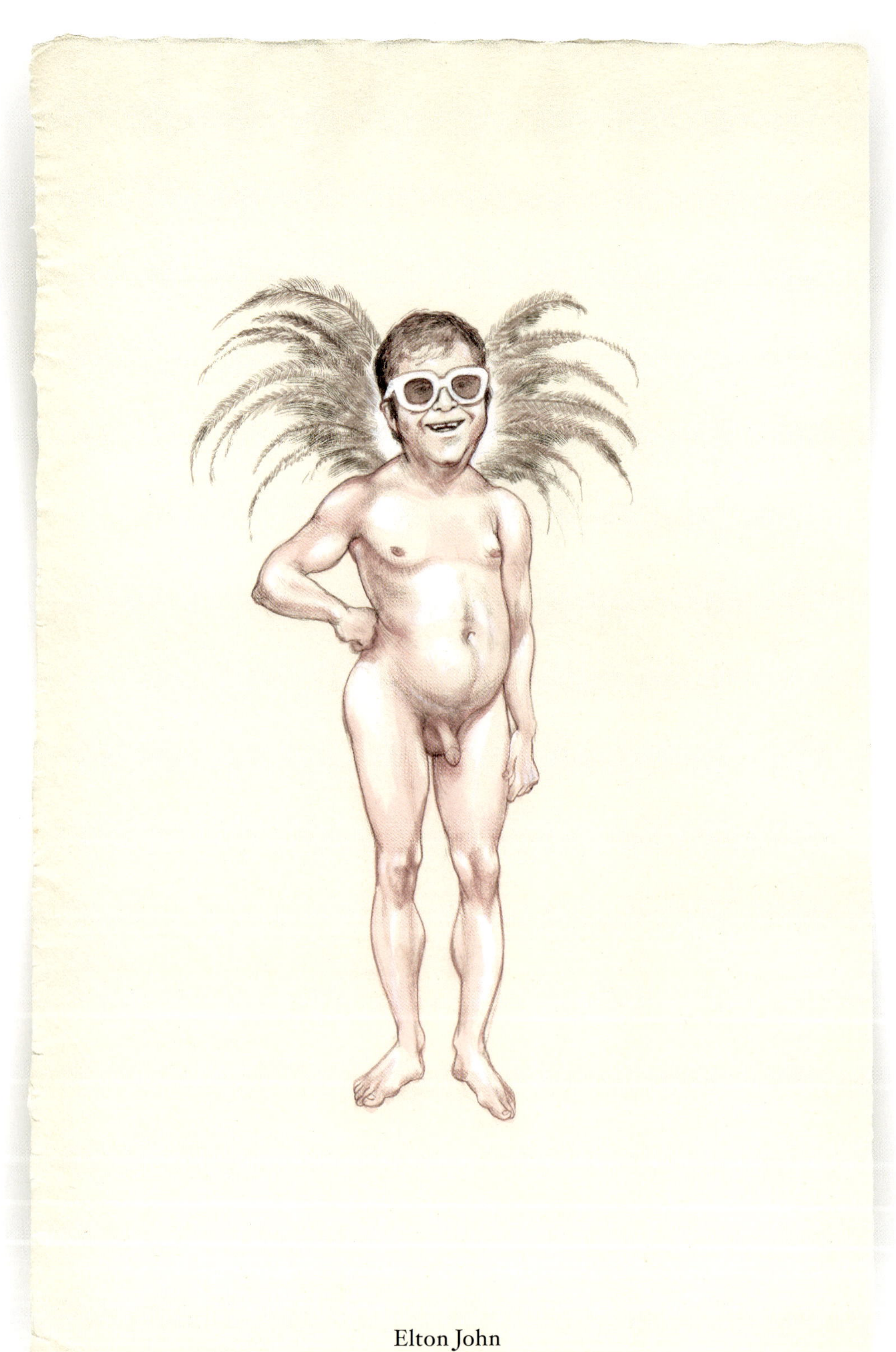

Elton John

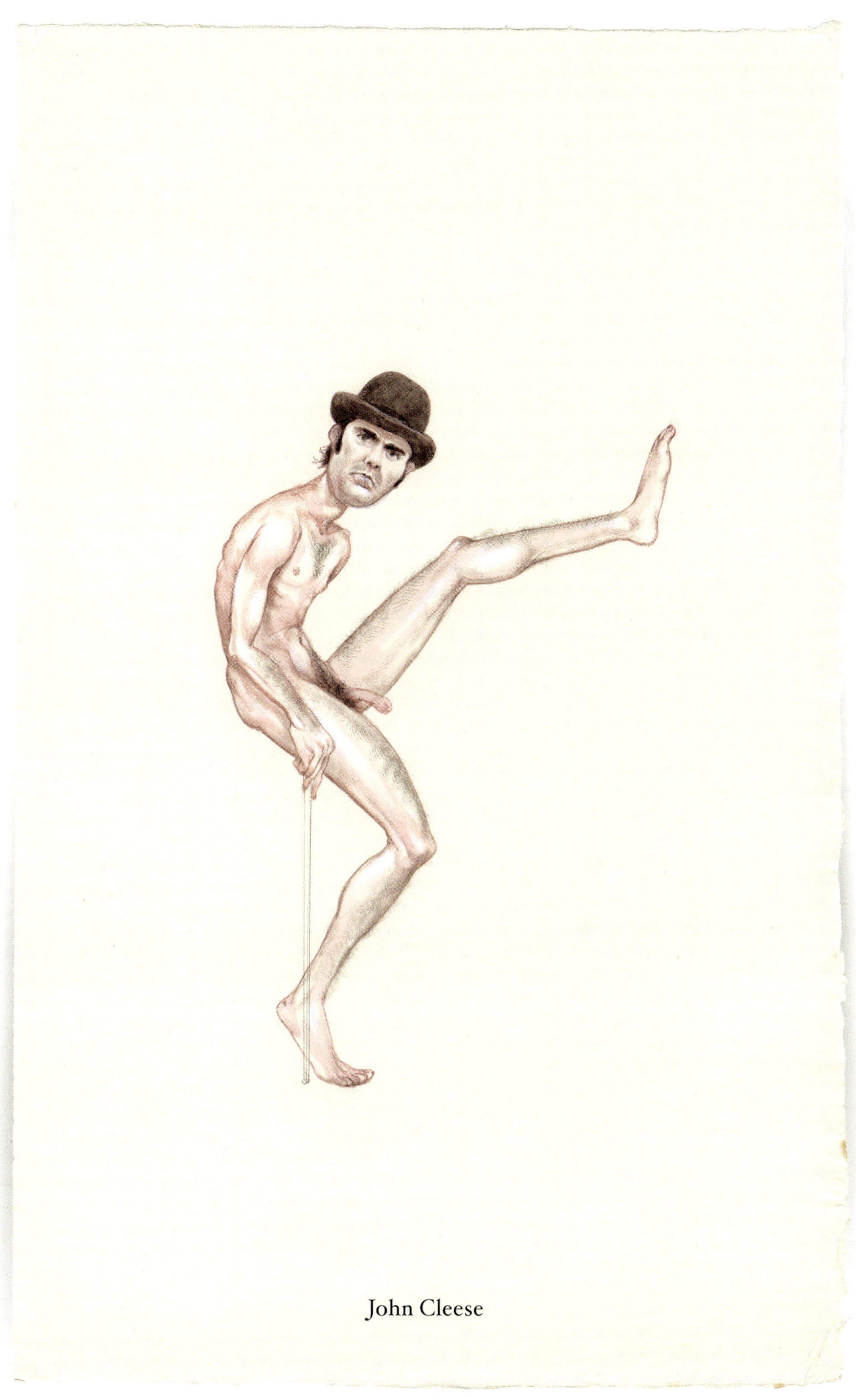

John Cleese

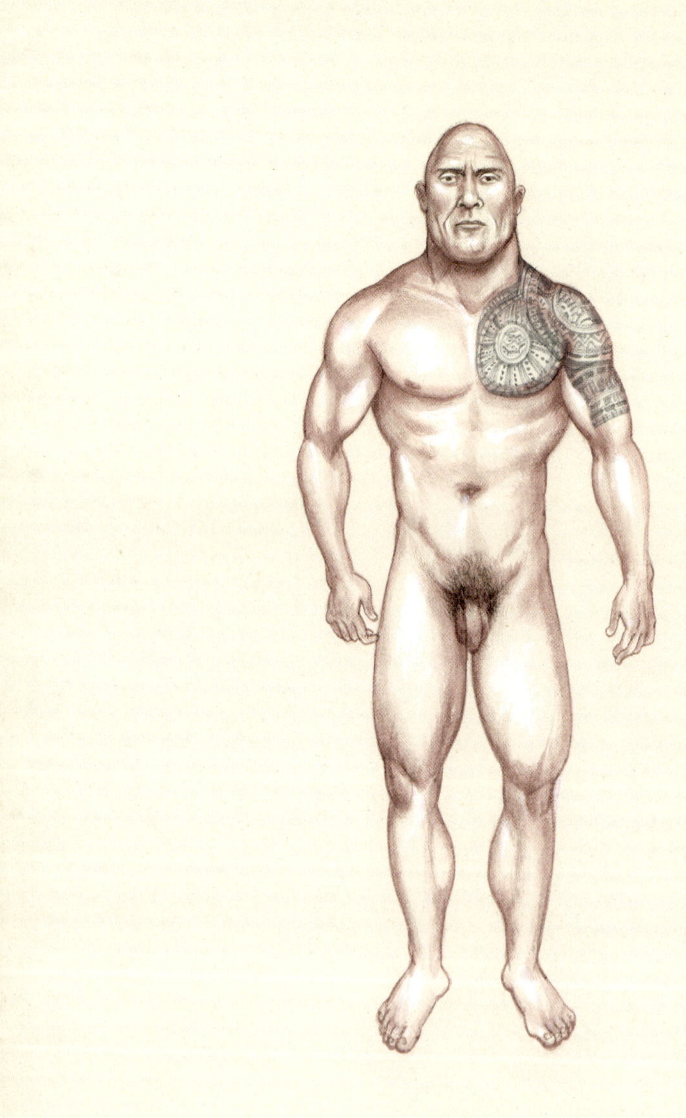

Dwayne Johnson

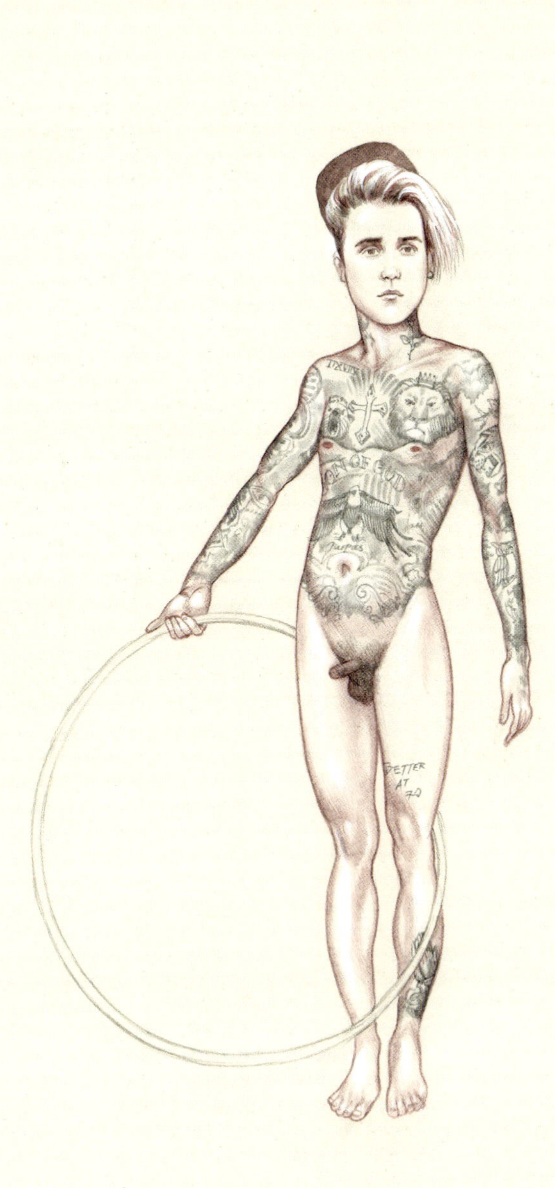

Justin Bieber

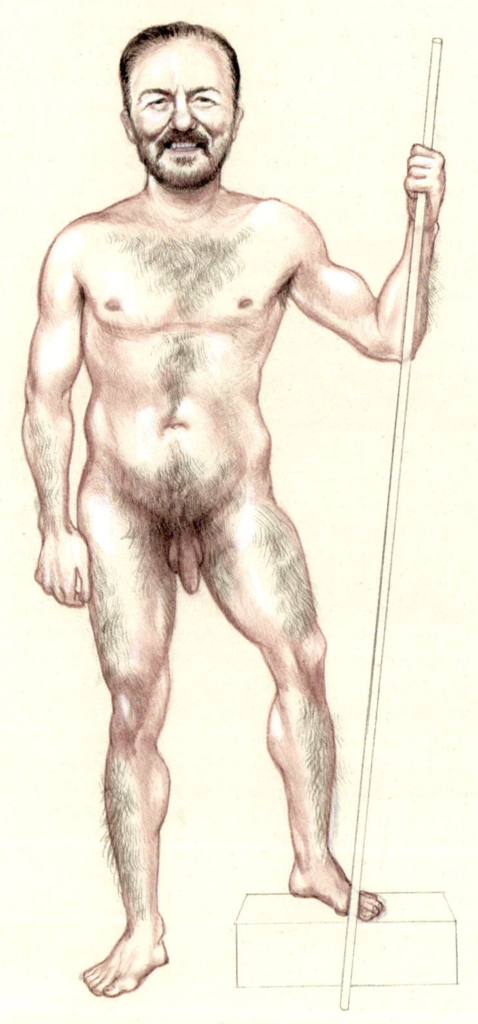

Ricky Gervais

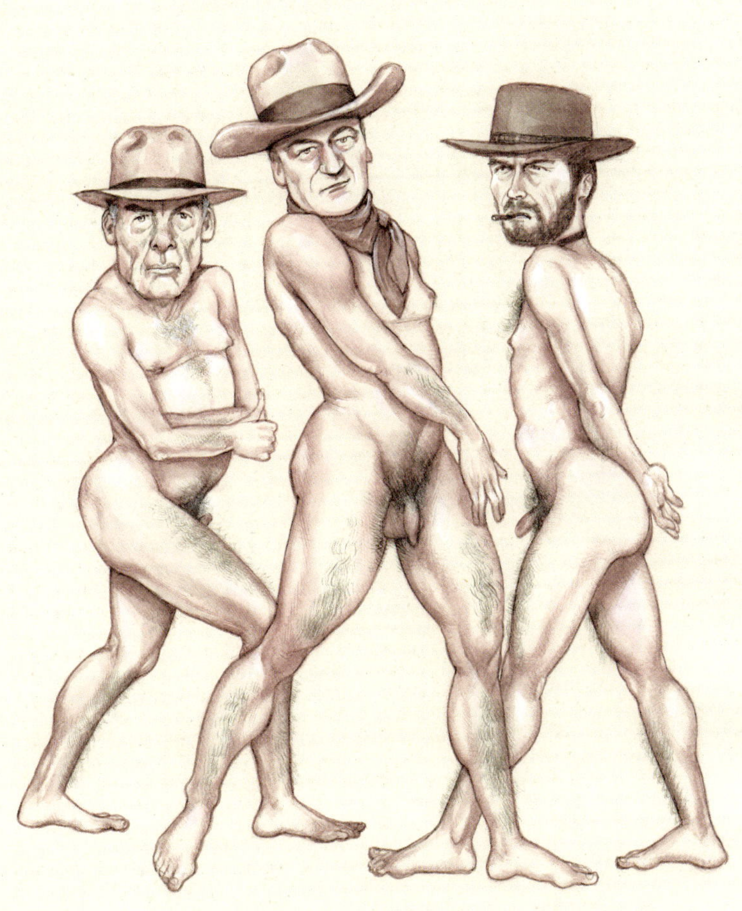

THE COWBOYS

Lee Marvin, John Wayne *&* Clint Eastwood

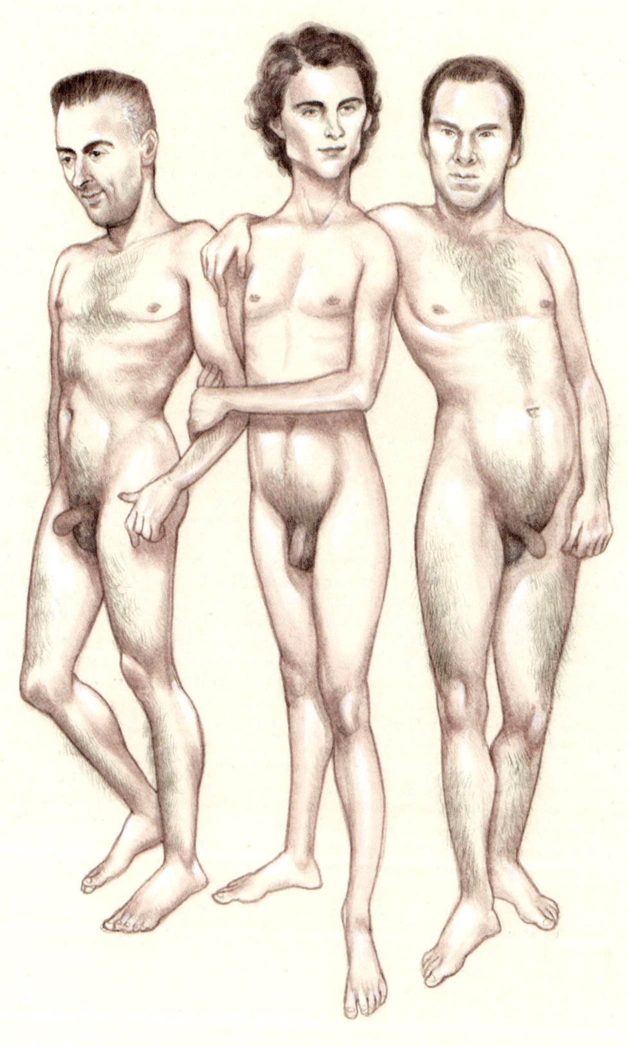

THE THESPIANS

Alan Cumming, Timothée Chalamet & Benedict Cumberbatch

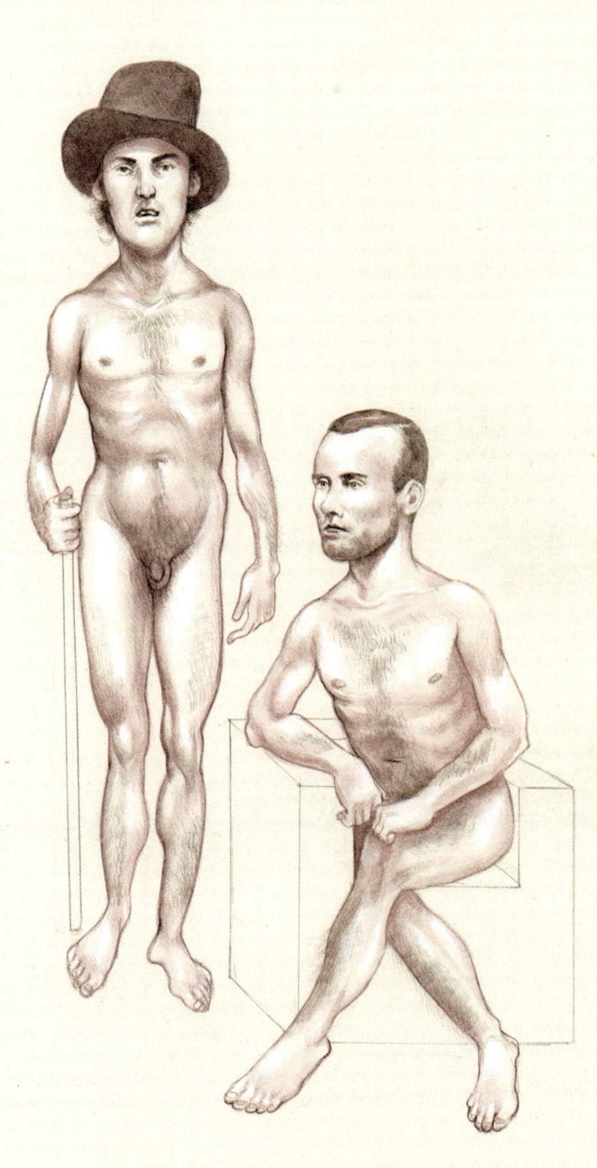

THE OUTLAWS

Billy the Kid & Jesse James

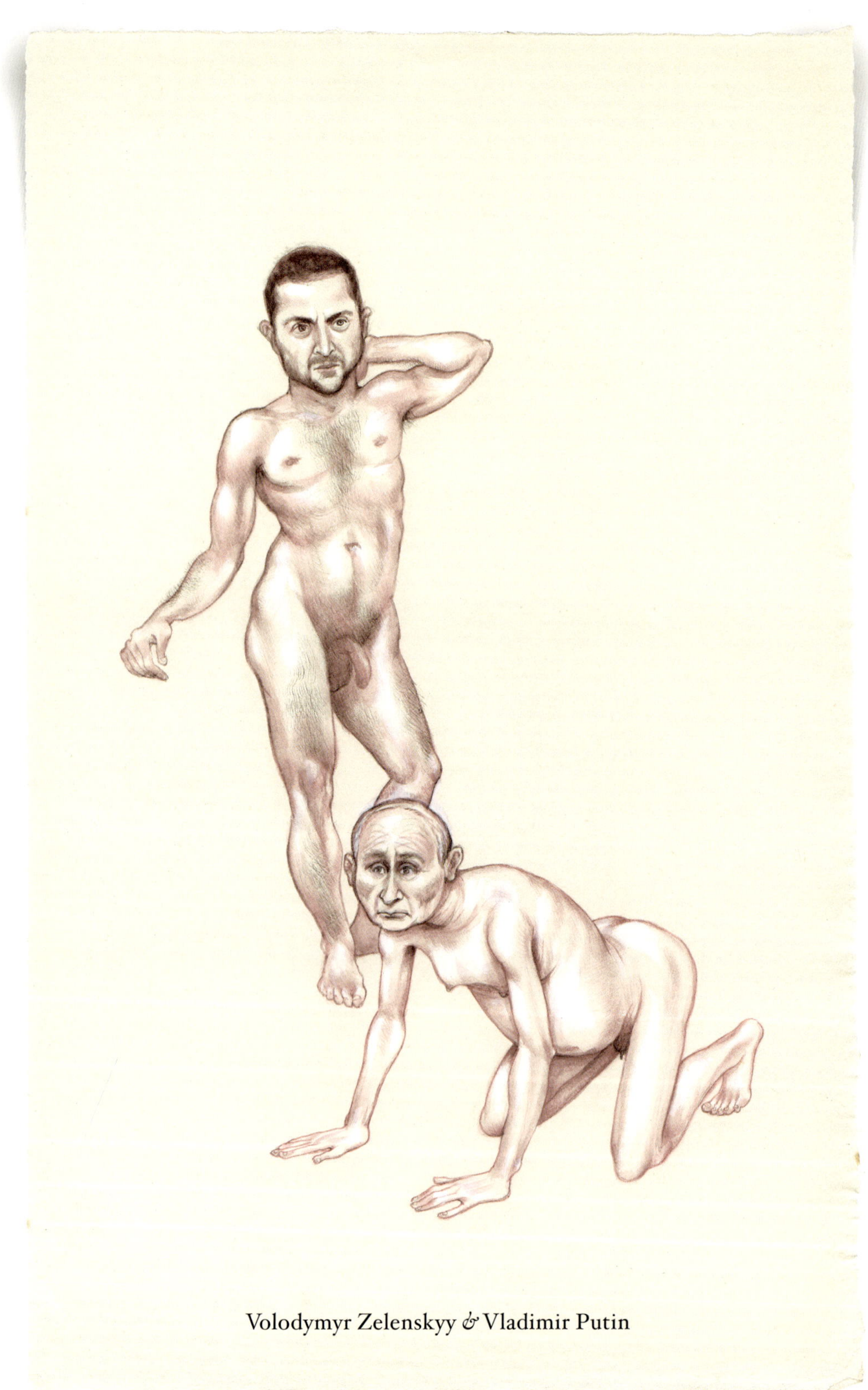

Volodymyr Zelenskyy & Vladimir Putin

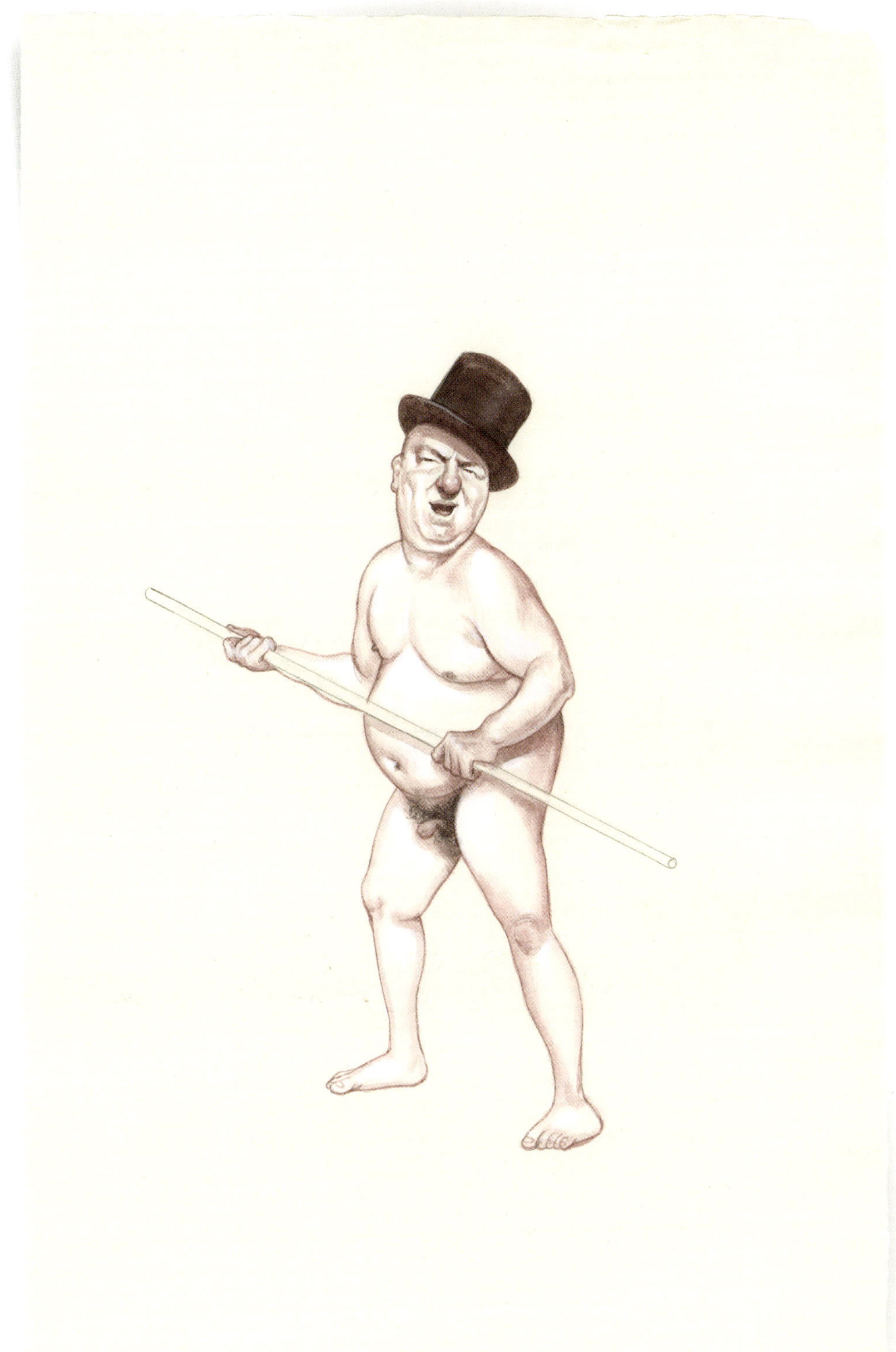

WC Fields

Canadian by birth, ANITA KUNZ has lived in London, New York and Toronto. Her socially and politically themed work has been published in major publications such as *Time* magazine, *Rolling Stone*, *Vanity Fair*, *The New Yorker*, *GQ*, *The New York Times*, *Newsweek*, *Sony Music*, *The Atlantic Monthly*, *Sports Illustrated*, and many others.

She has been honoured with many prestigious awards and medals and her critically acclaimed paintings and sculptures have appeared in galleries and museums worldwide including the Normal Rockwell Museum in Massachusetts, the Museum or American Illustration in New York City, and the Teatrio Cultural Association in Rome Italy.

Her works are in the permanent collections at the Library of Congress, The Canadian Archives in in Ottawa, The McCord Museum in Montreal, The Museum of Contemporary Art in Rome, and a number of her *Time* magazine covers are in the permanent collection at the National Portrait Gallery in Washington DC.

In the fall of 2003 she was the first Canadian and the first woman to have a solo show at the Library of Congress Swann Gallery in Washington DC.

She was inducted into the Royal Canadian Academy of the Arts in 2009. That same year she also received the Hamilton King award of excellence from the Society of Illustrators Museum of American Illustration for best illustration of the year.

She was inducted into the American Museum of Illustration Hall of Fame in 2017. Also in 2017, The Toronto Arts and Letters Club gave her the JEH MacDonald award. In 2018, Canada Post released a postage stamp honouring her work. And in 2022 she received the Gerald Scarfe prize from the Museum of the Avant-Garde in Switzerland.